MEMORIES OF DUKE

THE LEGEND COMES TO LIFE

Duke received this medal for his heroic surfboard rescue of eight drowning fisher-men off Newport Beach, California, in 1925. To capitalize on his fame, Paramount released this photograph to publicize Duke's 1925 movies, including Adventure, Lord Jim, *and* Pony Express.

MEMORIES OF DUKE

THE LEGEND COMES TO LIFE

Duke Paoa Kahanamoku, 1890-1968

With a Foreword by
Nadine Kahanamoku

Sandra Kimberley Hall
and
Greg Ambrose

The Bess Press
P. O. Box 22388
Honolulu, HI 96823

Design:
Bryant Fukutomi

Cover photos:
Front, top: Duke Kahanamoku surfing at Waikīkī, ca.
1915, photo by Gurrey, courtesy Hawai'i Maritime Center
Front, left: Duke Kahanamoku in 1930, courtesy Bishop
Museum
Front, center: Duke Kahanamoku on catamaran, courtesy
Honolulu Star-Bulletin
Back cover: Duke Kahanamoku statue, Waikīkī, photo by
Carlos Viti

A Note on the Sources:

Unless attributed to another source, quotations are from
interviews by the authors. Letters and radio and television
transcripts are from the Hawaii State Archives.

Although most published sources did not use diacritical
marks in Hawaiian words, they have been added here for
accuracy of meaning and consistency of text. Where
"Hawai'i" appears in the name of an organization, we have
used the spelling preferred by that organization.

Every effort has been made to trace the ownership of all
copyrighted material in this book and to obtain permission
for its use.

Cataloging-in-Publication Data

Hall, Sandra Kimberley.
    Memories of Duke : the legend comes to life :
Duke Paoa Kahanamoku 1890-1968 / by Sandra
Kimberley Hall and Greg Ambrose ; with a
foreword by Nadine Kahanamoku.
            p.   cm.
        Includes index and illustrations.
        ISBN 1-57306-020-8
1. Kahanamoku, Duke, 1890-1968
2. Hawaiians-Biography. 3. Hawaii-Biography. 4.
Swimmers-Hawaii-Biography. 5. Surfers-Hawaii-
Biography. I. Ambrose, Greg. II. Title.
DU627.7.K34.K55 1995   996.903-dc20

Printed in the United States of America
ISBN: 1-57306-020-8

Table of Contents

Mahalo Nui Loa/Aloha Nui Loa

SANDRA K. HALL:

A book like this, of memories, text, and photographs, could not be written without the assistance of hundreds of people. We are aware that there are others who have important insights into Duke's life and times whom we were unable to contact, for a variety of reasons, ranging from ignorance to the clock ticking. Please forgive us if we failed to contact you. Please contact us. We would like to share more memories of Duke in another volume. The more people who know about Duke, the more his aloha will be shared.

We say "Mahalo" to these colleagues, researchers, and friends for their assistance:

Photographs

International Swimming Hall of Fame, Buck Dawson, Executive Director Emeritus, Hall of Fame; International Swimming Hall of Fame, Preston Levi, Director, Research Services, Henning Library; International Surfing Hall of Fame, Ann Beasley; Library of Congress, Prints and Photographs, Jennifer Brathovde, Reference Specialist; Kamehameha Schools/Bishop Estate, Janet Zisk, Archivist, Luryier "Pop" Diamond; AP/Wide World, Jorge Jaramillo; Camera Hawaii, Kiyo Makamura; LeRoy Grannis, surfing photographer; Easter Seal Society, Billie Gabriel-Zito, VP/Development; United Airlines, Barbara Hanson, Corporate Communications Center; Pacific Aerospace Museum; The Academy Foundation/National Film Information Service, Margaret Herrick Library, Janet Lorenz, Librarian; Roland J.C. Pang, J C Photo Lab; Wilber Bergado Photography; Valerie Lees, Stephen Lees; William Blake; Elmar Baxter; Rick Reif.

Research and other assistance

In Hawai'i:
Bishop Museum Archives, DeSoto Brown; Hawaii State Archives, Geoffrey A. White, Richard R. Thompson; Outrigger Canoe Club, Historical

Committee, Eugenia McMahon; Outrigger Duke Kahanamoku Foundation, Earl Maikahikina-pāmaikalā Tenn; Hawaii Newspaper Agency, Bea Kaya, Librarian; Hawai'i Maritime Center, Stan Melman, Librarian; University of Hawai'i-Manoa, Hamilton Library, Hawaiian/Pacific Collections; Hawaii State Library, Hawaii Kai Branch; Hawaii State Library, Hawaii and Pacific Room; Hawaiian Historical Society, Barbara E. Dunn, Librarian; Kenneth Kuokoa Spicer; City/County of Honolulu, Municipal Reference and Records Center; Hawaiian International Billfish Tournament, Peter S. Fithian and Michael Nelson; Kona Historical Society Archives; Dr. George S. Kanahele; Joann Kahanamoku-Sterling; Mission Houses Museum, Judith A. Kearney, Librarian; Campbell's Instant Copy, Koko Marina; Hawaii Calls, Inc.; Dr. Sheenagh M. Burns; Derek Glaskin; Steve Brennan; Dr. Será Hoyt; Paul Kendall; Diane McGregor; Brad Smith.

In the mainland United States:
Ellen Briscoe, Assistant Director/Library, National Geographic Society; Time Warner Inc., Lany McDonald, Research Library Director; Library of Congress, Newspaper and Current Periodical Room, Frank Carroll, Serials Librarian; Library of Congress, Congressional Reference Division, Catherine A. Jones, Chief; Library of Congress, Motion Picture Division; Barbara Semonche, Librarian, School of Journalism and Mass Communication, University of North Carolina, Chapel Hill; Santa Barbara Surf Museum, James O'Mahoney; Tom Sena, Rockaway Beach, New York; Ken Erdman; Chicago Athletic Association, Theresa Lucas; Los Angeles Athletic Club, Richard "Duke" Llewelyn, George Guevara, Archivist; Patricia Henry Yeomans; Ron White, Chicago; *Houston Chronicle,* Sherry Adams, Librarian; Dr. Lawrence Clark Powell; Elaine Raines, Librarian, *Arizona Daily Star;* Jean Stuart; Field Museum of Natural History; Yale University Archives; University of Pennsylvania Archives; Amateur Athletic Foundation, Sports Library; Sheraton Hotels, Barbara Sheehan; Ellen Paris; Elizabeth J. Maggio; Ray Evans; Gerald D. Brown, *St. Louis Post-Dispatch*, Reference Library; Barbara Dantzler; Margaret H. Scott, Frank E. Johnson.

Overseas:
International Olympic Committee Archives; Paul McKay, General Manager, Harbord Diggers Memorial Club; Jennifer Broomhead, State Library of New South Wales; Alan Atkins, National Director, Australian Surfriders Association; Freshwater Surf Life Saving Club, Richard Ware, Kevin Nixon, Alf Henderson; Dr. Richard Cashman, Dept. of Sports History, University of New South Wales; Jack Finlay, coordinator, SurfWorld Australia; John Morcombe, *Manly Daily*, Librarian; Heather Rose; Maureen Wall; Marjory Sirks; Maureen Smith, Local Studies Librarian, Manly Municipal Library; Sue Brown, Local Studies Librarian, Warringah Shire Library, Dee Why; Peter Troy, Australian Surfriders' Association Archivist; New South Wales Amateur Swimming Association; Victoria Amateur Swimming Association; Kris Price; Carol Hall; Meg Smith; Jocelyn Price; Carol Gistitin and Leo Tidey, Special Collections, University of Central Queensland, Rockhampton Campus; Gail Hesselman; W.G. Marshall, Cronulla Surf Life Saving Club; *St. George and Sutherland Shire Leader*; Sutherland Library, Local Studies Librarian, Helen MacDonald; Waverley Library, Local Studies Librarian, Marion Curry; *Northern Beaches Weekender; Sydney Morning Herald;* Owen and Raie Kimberley; Linda Bottari.

GREG AMBROSE:

Special *mahalo* to the charming and enchanting Nadine Kahanamoku; Norene Elena Childress; Lindsey Keiki o ke Kai; George Downing; Rabbit Kekai; John Kelly; Clarence Maki; Fred Hemmings; Kimo Wilder McVay; Carlos Viti; Dennis Oda; Burl Burlingame; Bryant Fukutomi; Revé Shapard; Buddy Bess; John Flanagan; Dave Shapiro; Gerry Keir; Larry Fuller; and especially Sandra Kimberley Hall, who put her heart and soul into this book.

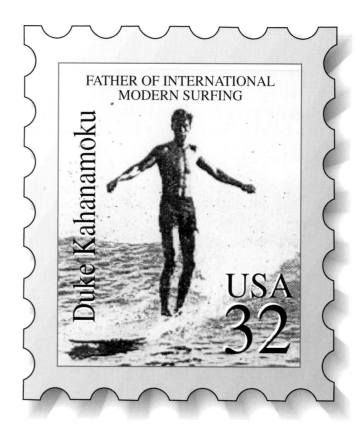

FATHER OF INTERNATIONAL
MODERN SURFING

Duke Kahanamoku

USA
32

Nadine was promised a postage stamp honoring Duke 30 years ago. The Hawai'i State Legislature passed a resolution in the 1980s requesting action, and author James A. Michener and former U.S. Senator Barry Goldwater lent their support, but still Nadine waits.

Currently, the International Surfing Hall of Fame is leading a petition drive for a postage stamp to honor Duke. Surfing magazines, such as *Longboard*, are rallying signatures. Ten thousand signatures are needed; 6,000 have already been collected. Send your name to Surfing Hall of Fame, P. O. Box 782, Huntington Beach, CA 92648, or write to Citizens' Stamp Advisory Committee, c/o Stamp Management, U.S. Postal Service, 475 L'Enfant Plaza, SW, Room 447E, Washington, DC 20350-2137.

Foreword

Nadine Kahanamoku has led a life that most people don't even dare to dream. A child piano prodigy and later a dancer, she ended her first marriage with enough money to travel by herself to the exotic places of the world. She met people famous and aristocratic. But her greatest adventures came after she married a Hawaiian man with a royal name and a heart of gold: Duke Kahanamoku.

And she has a message to pass on:

As a schoolgirl I had seen his picture in a movie magazine with Douglas Fairbanks and his wife. I saw this photograph and I fell in love with the picture of Duke.

When I met him, he was more wonderful than I had imagined.

I've had a good life, and I hope that when you read this book you enjoy it and get a feeling for Duke and me and the kind of life we shared together, and that you understand what made us tick. I was so in love, so terribly in love with him.

Highlights of Duke's Remarkable Life

1890	August 24, born in downtown Honolulu. First surviving child of Duke and Julia, full-blooded Hawaiians
1893	Family moved to Waikīkī's Kālia area
1896	Enrolled in first grade at Waikīkī-kai elementary school
1899	*Kāhili* bearer at Princess Kai'ulani's royal funeral
1903	Transferred to Ka'ahumanu elementary school
1904	Entered Kamehameha School for Boys
1908	Member of Kamehameha School's championship soccer team
1910	Transferred to McKinley High School
1911	Broke 3 freestyle world records in his first races, in Honolulu Harbor
1912	Won Olympic gold medal and set world record for 100-meter freestyle, Stockholm; also won a silver medal on the 4 x 200-meter freestyle relay team
1912	Introduced surfing to U.S.'s Atlantic Coast
1914-15	Introduced surfing to Australia and New Zealand
1915-1932	Helped popularize swimming and surfing in California
1918	Swam in exhibitions in about 30 mainland cities to raise money for Liberty Bonds for U.S. war effort. Boosted popularity of swimming. Reinforced reputation of Hawai'i as pre-eminent in swimming—through the next decade
1920	Recommended surfing as an Olympic event
1920	Antwerp Olympics, gold medals in 100-meter freestyle and 4 x 200-meter freestyle relay, fourth place in water polo
1924	Paris Olympics, silver medal in 100-meter freestyle
1922-1930	Lived in Los Angeles. Played small parts in about 30 movies
1925	Heroic board rescue of 8 drowning men at Newport Beach, California
1929?	Rode a monster wave 1-1/8 miles at Waikīkī, probably the longest ride in modern times
1932	Los Angeles Olympics, awarded bronze medal as alternate on the U.S. water polo team
1934	Elected City and County of Honolulu Sheriff. Re-elected 12 times
1940	August 2, married Nadine Alexander
1956	Official representative at Melbourne Olympics
1960	Sheriff position abolished when Hawai'i achieved Statehood and government reorganized. Appointed Hawai'i's Ambassador of Aloha
1963	Third visit to Australia to judge surf races
1964	Official guest at Tokyo Olympics
1965	First person inducted into both the Swimming Hall of Fame and the Surfing Hall of Fame
1965	First annual Duke Kahanamoku Invitational Surf Meet, Sunset Beach
1968	January 22, died in Honolulu; Waikīkī beachboy funeral
1969	Plaque and bust dedicated at Huntington Beach, California
1984	Posthumously inducted into U.S. Olympic Hall of Fame
1990	Statue dedicated at Waikīkī on centennial of his birth
1990	Duke Kahanamoku Way dedicated at Rockaway Beach, New York
1994	Statue dedicated at Freshwater, Sydney, Australia
1994	Biarritz, France, Surf Festival named in his honor
1994	First name inscribed in the Huntington Beach Surfing Walk of Fame
1994	Identification plaques placed on Waikīkī statue on his birthday

Introduction

Much has been written of the accomplishments of Duke Paoa Kahanamoku, the handsome Hawaiian swimmer who captivated the sporting world with his Olympic gold medals and who gave the gift of surfing to so many thousands of people across the oceans.

But all that has been written has been merely a recounting of Duke's accomplishments. This book is different, in that through the adroit arrangement of excellent photographs with insightful anecdotes, Duke emerges as a real person.

As you read this book, you will come to know the Duke who won the heart of everyone he met, and by the end of this book, you will be certain that had you met the Duke, you would have made a friend for life. And then you will know why loving hands drape leis upon Duke's statue on Waikīkī Beach daily. It's because Duke's aloha lives forever.

Holo A I'a

Almost 22 when he won his first Olympic gold medal, Duke represented the United States in the Olympics for 20 years, winning not only medals but the hearts of people all over the world. He is remembered as a swimmer not just for his remarkable speed, but for his grace in the water, his good humor, and his sportsmanship.

One of the most thrilling sights earlier this century was seeing Duke poised ready to hit the water for a race. As incredible as it sounds, sometimes as many as 40,000 people watched him race.

Earl Maikahikinapāmaikalā Tenn, Mrs. Duke Kahanamoku's personal representative on the Outrigger Duke Kahanamoku Foundation Board of Directors, commenting on Duke's Olympic career:

"Most Olympic swimmers compete in their first Olympics as teenagers and retire well before they are 30. Duke was an exception. He was unusually old to be an Olympian. He competed in his first Olympics and won his first gold medals at age 22. He competed in Olympics until he was 42, with qualifying times as good as or better than those of his younger days. His span of 21 years of Olympic participation is not likely to be beaten in aquatic sports or perhaps any sports."

Hawai'i residents were very proud of Duke's accomplishments. He was Hawai'i's first Olympian. Duke won these medals, cups and trophies at national and foreign meets between 1911 and 1913. Displays like this were frequently set up in Honolulu store windows.

Duke makes a splash that is heard around the world, August 12, 1911:

This was the first Amateur Athletic Union (AAU)-sanctioned event in Hawai'i's history. Without AAU recognition, swimmers could not compete on the mainland and be eligible for the Olympics. Since Honolulu had no adequate swimming pool, and Waikīkī was too far away, the races were swum in Honolulu Harbor at the piers where the ocean-going boats normally docked. Bleachers were set up on the wharves for the spectators.

Duke's startling performance—clipping more than 4 seconds off the 100-yard freestyle world record and more than a second off the 50-yard freestyle—though disallowed, propelled him to national press, mainland swimming meets, and then the Olympics, less than one year later. He would reign as World Champion for a decade.

Because Duke demolished the world record, rather than just shaving it by a fraction of a second, the press sought out the new champ. The fact that it was the first race he had competed in, and that he had never been taught or trained, added to his appeal.

In an interview reported in the August 20 *Pacific Commercial Advertiser*, the reporter played up the fact that Duke swam too fast to be photographed.

"On his first try at photographing Duke swimming his fastest, the photographer failed completely. On the second try, he pointed the camera at the horizon and was more successful. The plate shows one arm out of the water with the shark-like form dim beneath the waves. By the time the arm was back by the side, the body was shot out of the focus of the camera."

The reporter correctly predicted that the officials at AAU headquarters in New York would be skeptical when they heard about the record set by this "South Sea Islander."

The citizens of Hawai'i passed the hat to raise money to send Duke and three others to the mainland to compete in the nationals, and hopefully for two of them to get places on the Olympic team.

The *Pacific Commercial Advertiser* (April 9, 1912) described the 21-year-old Duke on his San Francisco arrival in 1912:

"He is an elongated looking Hawaiian standing 6 feet 2 inches and weighing 183 pounds. He has the build that denotes speed. He uses a swimming stroke . . . that he has invented himself." In describing the world record Duke had set 8 months previously, the reporter expressed amazement that when the course was resurveyed it was found to be 1 foot 5 inches OVER the distance.

On this, his first trip away from Hawai'i, the pressures began that would be lifelong—excel as a swimmer, survive scrutiny as a "Native," promote the Islands to attract tourists, and worry about money.

The *Pacific Commercial Advertiser* ran this letter from Duke written the night before he left New York for the 1912 Stockholm Olympics, with this editorial comment:

"Duke's letter shows his thoughtfulness for the friends and the land he left behind to conquer fresh laurels in the Old World. Duke is all right as a swimmer; he is all right also in his heart and aloha for Hawai'i."

> To The Editor of the Advertiser and People of Honolulu:
> One last word before leaving . . . for Stockholm. I am leaving the U.S. feeling fine and am in first-class condition, and further, expect to win.
> After returning from Stockholm, I desire to spend a week at the seashore riding the waves of the Atlantic Ocean on my surfboard, to show the good people of the U.S. how we Hawaiians ride the rolling billows at home in the Pacific Ocean. I shall then proceed with haste to good old Honolulu and you may rest assured that no matter how alluring the offers may be to induce me to stay in the States, I feel it my duty having left as an amateur to return as one.
> Trusting that I may soon return, bringing back with me that for which I was sent. I am very truly yours,
>
> Duke P. Kahanamoku

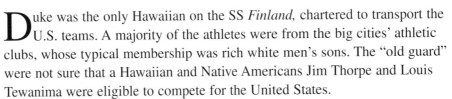

Duke was the only Hawaiian on the SS *Finland,* chartered to transport the U.S. teams. A majority of the athletes were from the big cities' athletic clubs, whose typical membership was rich white men's sons. The "old guard" were not sure that a Hawaiian and Native Americans Jim Thorpe and Louis Tewanima were eligible to compete for the United States.

On the 9-day trip, Duke "trained" as best he could in a makeshift canvas swim tank that was about 6 x 6 feet.

He said to Thorpe, "Jimmy, I've seen you run, jump, throw things [discus, shot, javelin] and carry the ball. You do everything, so why don't you swim too?"

Jimmy just grinned at [Duke] with that big grin he had for everyone, and said, 'Duke, I saved that for you to take care of. I saved that for you.'"

Tewanima won the silver in the 10,000-meter race. Thorpe dominated track and field, and Duke "took care of the swimming." Thorpe participated in 11 events and won both the decathlon and the pentathlon. "The greatest athlete of all time," said Duke.

(*Honolulu Star-Bulletin*, August 23, 1965)

By the standards of the time, the Stockholm Olympic swimming venue was quite modern; by today's standards, it was quite primitive. Swimmers often fouled each other unintentionally, as there were no lane markings. Since there were no chlorination and filtration systems, some swimmers developed excruciating ear infections.

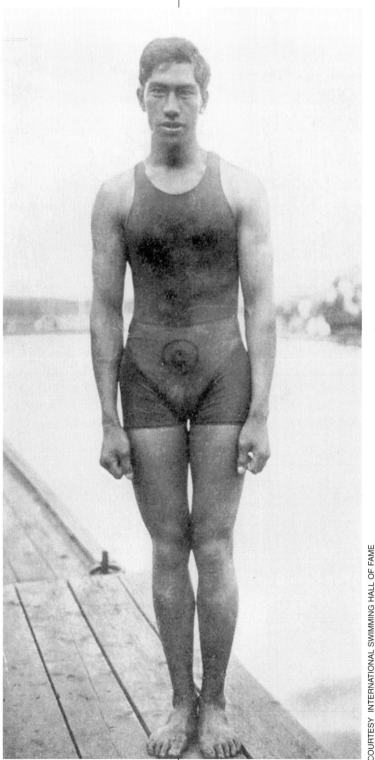

Duke kept his nerves under control by strumming his ukulele by the pool, "instead of biting my nails," he said. The competition was fierce, especially from Australian Cecil Healy, a medalist from the 1906 Games. Both Duke and Healy qualified for the final of the 100-meter freestyle.

Healy could have clinched the gold medal when Duke, bothered by the almost 24-hour-a-day sunshine, overslept, and did not show up for the final. Healy pleaded with the unsympathetic judges to give Duke a chance and to reschedule the race. They declined. Healy's refusal to swim forced the judges to relent. Duke won his first gold with Healy on his heels, 1-1/5th seconds behind.

This great act of sportsmanship cemented a deep friendship between the two rivals and between Duke and Australia.

"Brown swimmer was such a crowd pleaser, he was called to the Royal Box to be presented to the Queen," ran the headline. His trip to Sweden was a highlight of Duke's life. He was crowned with a laurel wreath by King Gustav V and his first Olympic gold medal was hung around his neck. The laurel head-lei became his lifelong most treasured possession.

(*Honolulu Star-Bulletin*, August 23, 1965, and *Houston Chronicle*, April 17, 1966)

July 1912, the new world champion, looking a little tense or tired, poses at the Stockholm Olympic pool. He became one of the most well known people in the world.

6

After being away for 9 months, Duke returned home—with a gold medal for the 100-meter freestyle, and a silver medal for the 4 x 200-meter relay. He had set a world record in Stockholm. He set a new record—an amazing 61-3/5 seconds—in Hamburg on his way home.

When the steamer *Wilhelmina* arrived at Honolulu Harbor, thousands of his friends welcomed him. As the Royal Hawaiian Band played and guns boomed, Duke waved his hat to the crowds.

When one of his friends yelled, "Luau tonight, Duke!" he dipped two fingers downward and back to his mouth, pantomiming the welcome prospect of eating his first poi in 9 months.

According to the October 1, 1912, *Honolulu Star-Bulletin*, Duke had "lost none of the modesty that won him hosts of friends everywhere he went. It only dawned on many of his fellow passengers who he was when the boat steamed into the harbor, though they had been together for 5 days at sea." Although he was splendidly received everywhere he went in Europe and on the mainland, he said that "the best part of his journey out into the big world had been his return to his home, friends, and family."

COURTESY BISHOP MUSEUM

The champ returned home after an absence of nine months. Suddenly a celebrity, and lionized wherever he went in Europe following the Stockholm Olympics, he was nevertheless so quiet and reserved on board the Wilhelmina *that many passengers were unaware who he was until the boat steamed into Honolulu Harbor to the piers crowded with Duke's fans and family.*

Years later, Duke was reunited in Stockholm with one of his competitors from the 1912 games.

For Pan American Airways inaugural service from New York to Norway, the public relations department conceived a brilliant strategy to guarantee widespread press coverage. Duke was the most popular American in Scandinavia, so he was invited to head the delegation of celebrities. The trip was extended from Oslo to Stockholm to ensure media coverage.

According to the *Advertiser*'s managing editor, Buck Buchwach:

"When Duke walked from the plane, the scores of cameramen and newsmen almost hid him from the rest of the crowd. Then a lanky bespectacled Swede stepped forward and gave Duke a bear hug that would have won any wrestling match . . . ."

COURTESY FOLKE HELLBERG

Arne Borg, a legendary Swedish Olympic swimmer, was Duke's friend for 50 years. Some of his greatest victories were in Honolulu and Australia. Borg and Duke were reunited in 1961 in Stockholm.

The enthusiastic greeter, whom Duke embraced just as warmly, was Arne Borg, the affable Swedish swimming superstar. They had been competitors at two Olympics.

After Duke was presented with the key to the city, "two super enthusiastic girls just lifted the husky Duke onto their shoulders to the delight of the crowd.

"'Just like it was here in 1912,' grinned Duke."

(*Honolulu Advertiser*, April 23, 1961)

◆

Five years after the Scandinavia trip and 55 years after the 1912 Olympics, Duke was recuperating in a Honolulu hospital from ulcer surgery. King Gustav's great-grandson, the 20-year-old heir to the Swedish throne, visited him. The Prince was touring the South Pacific as a Naval cadet. Hawai'i and Sweden's ties date back to 1852, when King Kamehameha III drew up trading and treaty rights. Duke and the prince perpetuated the treaty by trading caps.

COURTESY HONOLULU ADVERTISER

Duke, looking shaky and frail after ulcer surgery in March 1967, perked up for the visit of Carl Gustav, the 20-year-old heir to the Swedish throne. Carl was the great-grandson of King Gustav, whom Duke had met in Stockholm in 1912. They traded caps and stories before the prince headed for the surf at Waikīkī.

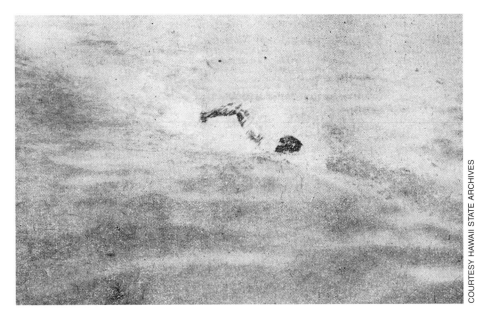

COURTESY HAWAII STATE ARCHIVES

Readers today might consider photos like this one quaint, but in pre-television days, this type of photograph showing the wake left behind by Duke's powerful kick was scrutinized by fascinated readers.

David Kahanamoku, closest to Duke in age of Duke's brothers, was a trainer for the 1924 U. S. Olympic swim team. In an interview in the September 1950 Outrigger Canoe Club *Forecast* about the origin of his brother's revolutionary swimming style, he said,

"In about 1910, Duke had watched some Australians swimming and bodysurfing at Waikīkī. He noticed that their style was different. They seemed to surge through the water with more power. The Aussies did the same overarm stroke (they called it the crawl) as Duke, but their leg movement was different.

"Duke like the rest of us swam with a self-taught frogleg movement. So he tried the Aussie straight leg kick, holding on to a surfboard, with his friend Frank Kalani. Since he found it somewhat unnatural, he modified it, with a slightly bent leg, which made his ankles and feet act like swimfins.

"In the 1912 Olympics, Duke showed his self-taught style's superiority by beating the Aussies. Then it was the Aussies' turn to watch and learn from him. Then they modified their Aussie crawl after he visited them Down Under! No wonder he always had a soft spot for Australia in his heart!"

COURTESY BURL BURLINGAME AIRCHIVE

Duke swam so effortlessly he was described as "half fish, half human." He excelled in all aquatic sports; the water was his home.

Honoluluans finally had the opportunity to see Duke swim against mainland swimming champs, at the 1914 Mid-Pacific Carnival.

Not one, but three surveyors measured the course in the Harbor at the Naval Dock at the foot of Alakea Street. The course was measured from moored pontoons in the Harbor where the competitors would start to a finish line in full view of the spectators. Anticipating that records would be set, the Geographical Survey's Chief Larrison verified the 440 yards, the 100 yards and the 50 yards course measurements to avoid a repetition of 1911.

Duke thrilled the crowd by winning the first race, the 440-yard freestyle. Then he set a world record in the 100-yard freestyle of 54-4/5 seconds, improving his own record by 2/5 of a second.

He was the Hawaiian and American record holder for the next race, the 50-yard freestyle. He took the lead for a fraction of a second, followed by George Cunha and Bob Small. Quick as a flash, though, San Francisco's Small pulled away, winning with a time that broke Duke's Hawaiian record by 1/5 of a second, and equaled the world record.

COURTESY BISHOP MUSEUM

Duke won friends with his sportsmanship, accepting his occasional defeats with grace. Here the announcement booms over the megaphone that Duke has been beaten by San Franciscan Bob Small, a relatively unknown swimmer, who looks surprised that he has beaten the 50-yard freestyle world champion in front of 6,000 of Duke's supporters at Alakea Slip, Honolulu Harbor.

COURTESY OUTRIGGER DUKE KAHANAMOKU FOUNDATION

In a previously unpublished photograph taken during Duke's Australian visit, Duke is easily recognized in the center. Next to Duke, to the left, is Francis Evans, team manager. George Cunha is second to the right of Duke. Next to Cunha (at end of row) is Manly swimming great Harry Hay, who was coach for a team of Aussies who visited Hawai'i 25 years later. A little Australian snobbery shows: the dignitaries are wearing suits. The photographer has gone to a great deal of trouble to position the men to his liking.

Australia had hoped to be crowned the world's best swimmers at the 1912 Games. Duke had demolished this dream. After Stockholm, feverish training began immediately for the 1916 Games.

The world champion was invited to visit Australia for three months to compete in the national championships and to travel interstate to demonstrate his revolutionary swimming style.

COURTESY OUTRIGGER DUKE KAHANAMOKU FOUNDATION

January 2, 1915, the 100-yard freestyle championship. Duke won in world record time—53-4/5 seconds. George Cunha came in second; Albert W. Barry came in third. Left to right, William Longworth, Duke, Ivan Stedman, B. Gordon Page, Barry, Cunha.

COURTESY HEATHER ROSE

Accompanying Duke on his eagerly anticipated trip to eastern Australia and New Zealand were world-class sprint swimmer George Cunha, age 19 (left), manager Francis Evans, age 23 (center), and Duke, age 24, the first foreign Olympian to visit Australia. The press called Cunha the world's finest "white" sprint swimmer, to differentiate him from Duke, "the dusky-skinned Islander." They were well matched and their finishes were hard to call, making it very exciting for the spectators. Evans, a second cousin to Queen Lili'uokalani, was a lifelong friend of Duke's. The photo is autographed by all three.

In just six years, Hawai'i was well established and respected in competitive swimming. The Hawai'i branch of the AAU was permitted to host the 1917 national championship. The 100-yard freestyle men's national championship headlined the meet. Six national champions arrived from the mainland to compete in what was described as "the greatest aquatic event in Hawai'i's history."

Duke usually swam freestyle sprints, but he also sometimes competed in breaststroke and the 220-yard freestyle. In the 220, Duke had been last to start. The national champ, Norman Ross, had the lead at 120 yards. By 200, Duke surged ahead. The crowd went crazy, throwing hats and cushions into the water. One fan threw a policeman into the water when the policeman ordered him to return to his seat. Ross said, "Duke deserves it and more. He is the greatest swimmer of all time . . . Duke knows how to win and how to lose. Tonight was his night and it is befitting that Neptune's favorite son should receive some real appreciation."

At meet's end, the tally showed 3 world records. Duke broke his own 100-yard freestyle record; in the first final of the 4 x 75-yard relay, the visiting swimmers and Honolulu teams swam to a dead heat in a world record. In the second final, the IAC won in an even lower new time.

(*Honolulu Star-Bulletin*, September 6 and 7, 1917)

All-star swimmers in Honolulu late August 1917 for the Labor Day meet. Left to right, back row: W. A. "Knute" Cottrell, Dorothy Burns, Claire Galligan, Duke, William Bachrach (manager of the women swimmers), Frances Cowells Schroth, unidentified person, Abe Siegel, David Kahanamoku, Norman Ross. Front row, left to right: Leslie Jones, Ruth Stacker, Bill Kiawe. Cottrell later became swim director at the Waikīkī Natatorium.

COURTESY BISHOP MUSEUM

A previously unpublished photograph from the 1917 championships. From the left, Duke, George Schroth, Norman Ross, William Bachrach, Frances Cowells Schroth and Stubby Kruger. The Schroths and Ross were all mainland champions. Bachrach later became Johnny Weissmuller's coach and manager.

Not surprisingly, swimmers from Hawai'i dominated the U.S. swim team at the 1920 Antwerp, Belgium, Olympics. (The 1916 Berlin Olympics were cancelled because of World War I.) With 7 representatives, Hawaiians came in first, second, and third in the 100-meter freestyle final. They won a total of 7 Olympic medals.

Duke reigned as world champion. He won a gold medal for the 100-meter freestyle and set a world record time of 60-2/5 seconds in the first of two finals. He also won a gold for the 4 x 200-meter relay team. He played on the U.S. water polo team, which came in a disappointing fourth.

After Antwerp, the team toured Paris, London, New York, Chicago, Detroit, San Francisco, and elsewhere, competing in 26 contests and bringing back 59 medals and other trophies.

Duke was mobbed wherever he went. In Paris, which he visited after the Antwerp Games, so many admirers surrounded him that the police had to clear a path. To protect him from the young women who tried to (and often succeeded in) kissing him, a chaperone accompanied him whenever he appeared in public.

In Detroit, one man drove 146 miles just to see Duke swim. Bill Harris, bronze medalist to Duke in the 100-meter freestyle, wrote home, "Mainlanders know little about Hawai'i. I have come to believe that all they do know is that it is the place where Duke Kahanamoku comes from."

(*Honolulu Advertiser*, November 10, 1920)

COURTESY INTERNATIONAL SWIMMING HALL OF FAME

Duke and his fellow Hawaiian teammates helped keep morale high on the rusty former troop ship Princess Matoika *en route to the Antwerp Olympics. The Hawaiians had a portable gramophone and played records for dancing. Duke also sang and played his ukulele. In Antwerp, Margaret Woodbridge, right, won the silver medal in the 300-meter freestyle, the only time this distance has been an Olympic event.*

Today's Olympians would be astonished at the canvas "pool" the swimmers were expected to train in on the Princess Matoika. The swimmers wore a harness and virtually swam in place against a clock for their allotted 10 minutes.

"A lot of people didn't know that Duke had a great sense of humor," said Olympic diver Hal Haig Prieste.

"Duke and I used to do a slapstick comedy routine on the streetcar on the way to the Antwerp pool.

"Duke was about a foot taller than me. We'd act like we were getting into an argument. He'd reach down and put his big hand over my face. I'd grab his wrist, then hang on and jump around. It looked like Duke was shaking me with one hand. Then I'd get away and chase him down the street."

(Bob Krauss, *Honolulu Advertiser*, June 1, 1982)

The 1920 U.S. Olympic swim team was dominated by Hawaiian swimmers. It was coached by Hawai'i's own George "Dad" Center. Their victories ushered in the golden age of Hawaiian swimming. The "pool" was a filthy, fenced-off canal, with a muddy bottom. Several swimmers nearly died of hypothermia from the freezing water. There were no hot showers. Here the U.S. relay gold medalists (left to right, Norman Ross, Pua Kealoha, Perry McGillivray, and Duke) are bundled up against the bitter cold.

According to the manager of a hotel where Duke, Warren Paoa Kealoha, and Norman Ross stayed, they established records that will stand for all time. He declared them the eating champions of the world.

"Mon dieu, they command ze bifstek with pommes frites, for three." Ross confiscated the whole platter, meant for three. Vegetables, ham and eggs, cheese, fruit, and desserts followed in turn while the manager moaned. The manager was horrified that they did not drink wine. In the middle of their meat course, they ate a huge bowl of sweet chocolate.

When informed that the men were champion swimmers of the world, the head waiter said, "No, they are not sea lions. They are meat-eating tigers!"

(*New York Herald*, October 1920)

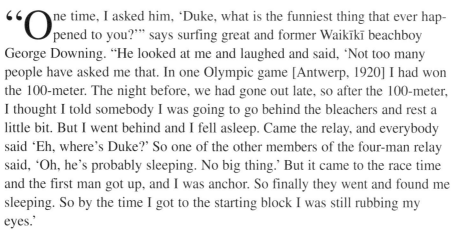

"One time, I asked him, 'Duke, what is the funniest thing that ever happened to you?'" says surfing great and former Waikīkī beachboy George Downing. "He looked at me and laughed and said, 'Not too many people have asked me that. In one Olympic game [Antwerp, 1920] I had won the 100-meter. The night before, we had gone out late, so after the 100-meter, I thought I told somebody I was going to go behind the bleachers and rest a little bit. But I went behind and I fell asleep. Came the relay, and everybody said 'Eh, where's Duke?' So one of the other members of the four-man relay said, 'Oh, he's probably sleeping. No big thing.' But it came to the race time and the first man got up, and I was anchor. So finally they went and found me sleeping. So by the time I got to the starting block I was still rubbing my eyes.'

"And they broke the world record, because he was such a tremendous swimmer."

"**H**ey kid, want to go for a ride?"

"I was sitting on the edge of the pool, dangling my feet in the water, when Duke swam over and asked me. Of course I said yes. After all, he was the greatest swimmer in the world, and the star attraction of the meet!"

They swam tandem—Aileen Riggin (Soule) provided the arms—Duke the feet. Soule swam overarm, Duke placed his hands on her waist. With his powerful kick, they zoomed across the water "like a power boat." This was 1918. She was a petite 65-pound 12-year-old, just learning to swim. He was swimming in New York City for the U.S. Liberty Bonds campaign.

"That is the fastest I have ever moved across water in my life!" said Soule, herself a two-time Olympian.

"He was always like this with young people—always pleasant, encouraging, like a big brother."

Echoed Ethelda Bleibtrey, "He was like a father to us at the 1920 Games."

Now a Waikīkī resident, Soule, 89, is probably the oldest living American who knew Duke at an Olympics. She was Duke's fellow team member for both the 1920 and 1924 Games.

PHOTO BY SANDRA K. HALL

Aileen Riggin Soule, now 89, is one of the world's oldest Olympic gold medalists. She was the first woman to win medals in both diving and swimming and starred in the first swimming training movie, in 1922. She later turned professional, starring in Billy Rose's Aquacade extravaganza, and acted in movies.

Duke was a hero to Helen Wainwright (left) and Aileen Riggin. The three medalists had just returned from Antwerp and were part of the parade of Olympians in New York City. Aileen and Helen had to wear men's hats. They were too big for them, and hid their eyes. American women dominated the springboard diving. Aileen, age 14, won the gold, and Helen won the silver. Duke, Aileen, and Helen were teammates again in 1924.

COURTESY OUTRIGGER DUKE KAHANAMOKU FOUNDATION

The Paris Olympics of 1924 was 20-year-old Johnny Weissmuller's first Olympics. He was understandably nervous. In *The Complete Book of the Olympics, 1984/1992,* David Wallechinsky describes how Weissmuller, stepping up to the starting block for the 100-meter freestyle final, did a double-take. Next to him on one side was the defending champion, 34-year-old Duke, and on the other, 21-year-old Sam Kahanamoku. Weissmuller wondered if the brothers had planned to swim a team race against him to unnerve him.

Duke reassured him. "Johnny, good luck. The most important thing in this race is to get the American flag up there three times. Let's do it."

And they did. First, Johnny. Second, Duke. Third, Samuel.

Johnny Weissmuller and Duke at the pier on Weissmuller's arrival in Honolulu in 1922. It is possibly the first meeting of the 17-year-old Weissmuller and the 31-year-old Duke. They did not compete, since Duke went to Hollywood for movie auditions.

COURTESY HAWAII STATE ARCHIVES

In 1957 NBC television featured Duke in Ralph Edwards' *This is Your Life.* Weissmuller was one of the surprise guests. He said, "This bloke, this old guy, he taught me how to beat him!"

Weissmuller enjoyed embellishing and repeating this story for years. They were lifelong, close friends, which is quite unusual—the former champ and the one who usurped his title.

Although Weissmuller's record of the most national titles in U.S. swimming history still stands—36 from 1921-1928—he is remembered as the movie star, Tarzan, and the "guy who dethroned the Duke."

Kimo Wilder McVay, Duke's personal manager for the last seven years of Duke's life, remembers Duke commenting, years later, about the 1924 defeat, "Well, at least it took Tarzan to beat me."

These superstars have learned how to pose fetchingly for the camera. Left to right, Johnny Weissmuller, Aileen Riggin, Duke, and (kneeling) brother David Kahanamoku, who accompanied the 1924 swim team as a trainer and masseur.

On Valentine's Day 1930 Duke gave swimming demonstrations at a meet named in his honor at the Waikīkī War Memorial Natatorium. He was described as the king of all swimmers in the world, and king of Hawaiian swimmers, when he swam 100 meters in under 1 minute, 59-4/5 seconds, at age 39-1/2.

His speed was improving with age—he thought maybe he could realistically try out for the 1932 Games in Los Angeles.

He did not make the team, but was an alternate for the bronze-medal-winning water polo team, and helped with training.

Duke, Clarence "Buster" Crabbe, Harold "Stubby" Kruger—all three from Hawai'i—and Johnny Weissmuller (Illinois) at the swimming tryouts for the 1932 Olympics, held in Cincinnati, Ohio. With them are race officials, Red Cross nurses, and Boy Scout helpers. Weissmuller won a total of 5 gold medals (for the 100-meter freestyle and 4 x 200-meter freestyle relay at the 1924 and 1928 Games, and a gold for the 400-meter freestyle in 1924).

This photo was circulated worldwide in anticipation of the 1928 national Olympic trials. Duke was considered "a safe bet" for the U.S. team. Unfortunately, he missed the 1928 Amsterdam Games because of illness. Four years later, he tried out for the 1932 team.

Swimming as an organized, competitive sport was so new earlier this century that it did not have a name. Duke was described in the press as a "natatorial expert," a "natatory athlete," or "a natationist"— from the Latin word "natare," meaning "to swim." A swimming pool was called a "tank," a "basin" or a "natatorium."

The words "swim" and "swimming pool" eventually became widespread, but there is still an old-style Natatorium in Waikīkī, a reminder of the past. It was erected to honor Hawai'i *nei*'s 101 World War I dead. Instead of a passive war memorial, it was a brilliant living memorial, a statement that the ocean that surrounds Hawai'i is very important to the fabric of the culture. Swimming brought Hawai'i international fame for four decades—Hawai'i dominated Olympic teams from 1912 to 1956. Swimming has been Hawai'i's most successful sport on the international arena.

One of Hawai'i's swimming pioneers, Judge William Rawlins, said "Opening the Natatorium without Duke would have been like having a luau without poi, leaving out the main ingredient, so to speak."

(*Honolulu Advertiser*, August 27, 1927)

The Waikīkī War Memorial Natatorium opened on Duke's birthday in 1927. Duke returned to Honolulu and swam laps to "christen" it at the official ceremonies. At the time, he was living in Hollywood and appearing in a vaudeville act. The Natatorium was considered one of the greatest saltwater pools in the world.

For 25 years, the 100-meter, saltwater Natatorium was one of the most popular places at Waikīkī. There, thousands learned to swim, learned lifesaving techniques, or watched the world's greatest swimmers compete. Now in disgraceful disrepair, it may yet win the dubious honor as the first war memorial listed on the National Register of Historic Places to be destroyed.

◆

Japan honored Duke as an official visitor to the 1964 Tokyo Olympics. He was seated in the Emperor's personal box, stayed in the best hotels, and had a personal chauffeur. The prime minister's daughter acted as interpreter. "Everyone knew Duke," Nadine reminisced. "They would come up to him, bow and say 'Hello, Duke,' very politely."

Thrum's *All About Hawaii Almanac* (1967) describes how Duke learned to swim:

"My father and uncle just threw me into the water from an outrigger canoe. I had to swim or else," Duke said. "That's the way old Hawaiians did it. I don't know exactly how old I was, but I was real young, three or four years old. I made it back to the boat okay. I think it was at Crescent Bay, which is what we used to call the Kālia part of Waikīkī Beach."

———————◆———————

Sportswriters and spectators were awed at how effortlessly Duke swam. "He swam like a fish. He was half fish, half man. He was a merman, a seal, a paddlewheel steamer." Eventually they ran out of suitable metaphors.

Nadine, "I always thought he looked like a dolphin—you know, born in the water."

Kenneth Brown, longtime friend of Duke's: "He was a man of the sea—he was at home there."

Sportswriter Carol Hogan placed Duke in his context for posterity: "It is unlikely there will ever be an all-around waterman the way the late Duke was."

(*Honolulu Advertiser*, August 22, 1979)

———————◆———————

"He loved the ocean," says surfing great and former Waikīkī beachboy George Downing. "The guy was like a fish. He was a big man, but when you'd see him jumping in the water, there was no big splash; he would just slip right in.

"He caressed the wave. The wave was something that he treated tenderly, . . . like handling a woman. When you saw him dive in, everything

Duke loved bodysurfing, water polo, surfboard water polo, fishing, paddling, and sailing, and he excelled at them all. Notice his enormous shoulders and arm span, which helped propel him through the water.

was sleek, blending with the water. When he rode a wave it was the same way. He seemed to seek out the energy of the wave and not do anything more than just be part of it.

"The ocean was special to him. That's why he moved so fast in it. He understood what made you move better; he flowed with it. This is why as a canoe steersman he could feel how the canoe was moving, what angle you had to put it in to move fastest. It's a gift, a gift that was part of the family. All the brothers were capable of this.

"He had a way of popping the water, too, and he taught all us guys to take our hands and make the water pop. I still do it today. We used to use that when we would surround fish; that's how we could scare fish into staying in the net when we would do *hukilau*."

◆

Ruth Wayson Stacker, herself a champion swimmer, concluded that Duke's ancestral links to the spirit world accounted for his phenomenal swimming ability.

"Every Hawaiian born into the world is presented with a particular fish god, be it the mullet, the eel, or the shark (*manō* . . . . The *manō* is [the Kahanamoku's] chief high god, their *'aumakua.* . . .

"Duke's father—Captain Duke . . . told me that it was because of the shark that Duke had such success. He told that he had the direct promise from the chief shark of Honolulu Harbor and Pu'uloa that in Duke's two favorite distances he never would be defeated.

"The Captain felt he had more pull than the average native because his own father had been high retainer for King Kamehameha."

(*Honolulu Star-Bulletin*, October 8, 1918)

One of Duke's widow's favorite photographs. Sculptors often referred to his having "the perfect athletic male physique."

Duke's birthdays became more special and more extravagant with every year of his seventh decade. The wire service noted his birthday each year. He was deluged with cards and letters:

After reading about Duke's 73rd birthday celebrations, Ernest M. Smith, a former San Francisco sports columnist, wrote,

"[Last time we met] was when you and I 'raced' for the Red Cross Benefit in Richmond, VA in 1918. You and 'Stubby' (Harold Kruger) were on tour.

"I had not been in the water for about 6 months, because my position as Infantry Captain gave me no chance to swim. When I told you what a joke the 100-yard race would be, you said, 'Ernie, it will be a great race!' And it was—because you let me take the lead for about 90 yards, and then you went on to win by a stroke, in the fabulous time of 58 seconds.

"I shall always recall this delightfully friendly gesture."

Duke knew, because he was Hawaiian, how important it was not to embarrass the captain in front of his men.

Every year after about his 60th birthday, Duke's birthday celebrations became more extravagant. One year he had a sand model of a cake on the beach with a live bathing-beauty centerpiece. Another year he was portrayed as a surfer on his cake. For his 74th birthday (above), held in the hot sun at the International Market Place, he was portrayed swimming at Waikīkī, with palm trees and Diamond Head. After a birthday hula, he was serenaded with a new song, "Duke Kahanamoku Is His Name."

Nadine remembers, "Duke told me that he swam to make the races look interesting. Give the spectators a thrill with an exciting finish. Also make his competitor look good.

"For decades there were rumors that he did not push himself, that he could have always tried harder. Maybe he could have. But that was Duke; he was always kind. If he didn't have the heavy swimsuit he probably would have made better time too. Today swimmers shave their heads and bodies. It's very different. How can you compare—the pools, the turns, the starting blocks, everything's different."

COURTESY KAMEHAMEHA SCHOOLS/BISHOP ESTATE

Duke with Los Angeles Athletic Club Olympian Ludwig "Ludy" Langer at Honolulu's 1916 Mid-Pacific Carnival. They had often competed in California swim meets and were real crowd pleasers. Ludy beat Duke in the 880-yard freestyle when Duke lost count of the number of laps he had swum. He heard a pistol shot and thought he had finished, but the shot was to signal the last lap. Later, Duke beat national champion Langer in the 440 yards to the crowd's delight. Duke once met a young boy in Australia who reminded him of Ludy. He placed his hand on the lad's head and said, "You're Ludy." The now 80-something gentleman had always thought his nickname must be Hawaiian, until the author told him about Langer.

The world's twenty greatest swimmers were inducted into the new International Swimming Hall of Fame, in Fort Lauderdale, Florida, in December 1965. And Duke's name was the first.

Three of the greatest swimmers in U.S. history—Duke, Johnny Weissmuller, and "Buster" Crabbe—at their induction into the International Swimming Hall of Fame. Besides their swimming fame, they also appeared in movies. Duke had small parts in about 30 movies, Johnny was the most famous Tarzan, and Buster was Flash Gordon and Buck Rogers.

He'e Nalu

Duke won medals, trophies, and worldwide fame as a swimmer, but he surfed purely for the fun of it in an era before surfing was a competitive sport. Although no spectacular video footage records his legendary longboard surfing, museums and memorials in Australia, California, Florida, New York, Hawai'i, and elsewhere pay tribute to his influence on surfers and the sport of surfing all over the world.

Four Hawai'i icons—Waikīkī, Diamond Head, Duke and a surfboard—in the 1930s. Duke is posing here with one of his many handmade surfboards. This is his 16-foot hollow redwood. Surfers kept massive boards like this at the beach, as they were too heavy and unwieldy to carry far or to load on top of a car.

In an interview when he was 76, Duke said that he learned to surf when he was 8 years old. "We *keikis* taught each other." Boards were highly prized by Hawaiians in ancient times and often passed down from generation to generation. Royalty surfed with the big *olo* boards, which is why surfing was called the sport of kings. Commoners used shorter boards, called *alaia*. Children of course used smaller bodyboards.

(*Houston Chronicle*, April 7, 1966)

◆

Unfortunately, there are few early photographs of the young Duke riding his surfboard. Cameras used plates, were slow, bulky, and heavy and needed tripods to stabilize them.

Over time, cameras became more compact, but it was not until the 1930s that the first waterproof camera was developed by Duke's close friend Tom Blake.

That is why most photographs of Duke are taken of him posing on the beach with his board.

COURTESY BISHOP MUSEUM

This previously unpublished photograph, slightly damaged and repaired, was taken at the Kūhiō Beach, Waikīkī, beach wall about 1918.

COURTESY HAWAI'I MARITIME CENTER

The original Hui Nalu Club at Waikīkī was formed for social and competitive surfing, swimming, and paddling. Membership was not exclusive; members could belong to other clubs as well. There are or have been Hui Nalu Clubs on every continent, modeled on the original. In this photograph are several famous aquatic stars referred to elsewhere in this book—Ethelda Bleibtrey, Hal Prieste, Ludwig "Ludy" Langer.

Q. "Your old Hui Nalu Club was probably the first surf club ever formed. Tell us how it got started."

Duke: "'Knute' Cottrell and I were out surfing one day . . . . We were sitting there, waiting for surf to come in . . . . We thought, Gee if we form a club, the name would be Hui Nalu, because *hui* is 'to get together,' or 'organization,' and *nalu* is 'surf'. . . .

"We'd meet at the trees and talk about the surf. We kept our boards under, or in the trees. Later we moved to under the shower tree on the Ala Wai Canal. Always a tree! Never a club house!"

(*Surfer*, March 1965, pp. 29-33)

When Duke showed Australians how to make a surfboard and ride it, he introduced one of the world's oldest sports, a sport that is at least 1,000 years old, to one of the world's newest countries.

Australians certainly knew about surfboard riding before Duke's visit. Then, as now, they were sports-obsessed, and no sport escaped their scrutiny. Boats en route from the United States to Australia stopped midway in Honolulu for at least a week, and travelers saw surfing at Waikiki. But the Aussie attempts to make their own boards were futile. They tried planks and doors. One well-known Sydney swimmer, Charles D. Paterson, even imported a board from Waikīkī in 1912. When he and his mates couldn't figure out how to ride it, his wife used it as an ironing board.

If you visit Sydney's Freshwater Beach today, people still talk about Duke's surfing demonstration as though it were recent, not eight decades ago.

Since Duke was unfamiliar with Australian timber, George Hudson, the largest timber yard in the southern hemisphere, helped Duke select an appropriate piece of timber for this surfboard. He chose sugar pine for its buoyancy. The board was transported around the beaches in the carriage drawn by the Creamy Ponies, a for-hire horse and buggy. The man in the rear is Donald D. McIntyre, a swimming official who helped arrange Duke's visit.

COURTESY HEATHER ROSE

Isabel Letham rode tandem with Duke several times in Australia, and became that country's first "Gidget." She was an outstanding ocean water swimmer, aquaplanist, and swimming instructor. A major force behind Australian monopoly of women's international surfing, she was an inductee of the Australian Surfing Hall of Fame. She died at age 95 in 1995. Her ashes are sprinkled at her beloved Freshwater.

COURTESY ISABEL LETHAM

Cecil Healy's mates arranged for Duke to spend Christmas 1914 at Boomerang, a Freshwater beach camp. For Australia, Duke's visit meant the birth of a new sport.

One spectator, the late Isabel Letham, in a December 1993 interview said she could still recall the day clearly: "To see Duke stand and do all sorts of tricks on a wave, and then, at the end to stand on his head—people couldn't believe their eyes."

The 15-year-old Letham, a fine bodysurfer and ocean swimmer, became Down Under's first surfer. When Duke asked for a partner, the burly life-savers "volunteered" her. She remembered how she paddled out with Duke through the pounding surf. He abruptly swung the board around and said, "Move back this way a bit. Kneel. Stand up. Now!"

She recalled that she froze, like a person being told to walk out on a plane wing in flight. Duke pulled her up by the scruff of her neck. The breaking waves were mountainous and it was "like looking down a cliff." After riding four more waves, she was "hooked for life. It is the most thrilling sport of all."

While Duke toured Australia's eastern states competing in swim meets, Letham practiced on his board. On his return she rode tandem with him again at a widely publicized exhibition at Dee Why Beach.

About the December exhibition, Duke wrote, in his book *Duke Kahanamoku's World of Surfing*, "I must have put on a show that more than trapped their fancy, for the crowds on shore applauded me loud and long . . . ."

He was brilliant and unforgettable, and an extraordinary teacher. Aussies became instant converts. Three of the young people in the crowd who hung on his every action became lifelong disciples. All are Australian Surfing Hall of Fame inductees: Justin "Snow" McAlister, 13 times national champion, Letham, and Claude West.

COURTESY HEATHER ROSE

The fascinated crowd followed Duke from the water after his first Australian surfing demonstration. Note the small board the youth walking next to Duke is carrying. Swimmers were very adept with small boards, and at bodysurfing, but riding larger boards had eluded them. Claude West described Duke's performance as "very agile. It was as though he had suckers on his feet."

COURTESY WARRINGAH SHIRE LIBRARY, DEE WHY

Duke carrying his board at Freshwater, Christmas 1914. Besides showing the eager Aussies how to fashion a board from a plank, Duke showed them how to cut across the waves instead of pointing the board toward the shore.

For hundreds of years, the Hawaiians called surfing by the beautiful and metaphorical name *he'e nalu,* "wave-sliding." Honolulu publications called it "surfing" or "surfboard riding." The Australian press was unsure what to call it. They called it "board shooting," "board walking" and "shooting the breakers."

COURTESY MAUREEN WALL

Duke and, probably, a reporter, at a beach during Duke's Sydney visit. Duke was very popular with the press. On many days he received more coverage than the war raging in Europe. The press analyzed his swimming and surfing styles and wrote about his lineage, his accent, and his curious musical instrument, "the euculale."

B esides demonstrating the fine points of surfing, Duke showed the Australians how to fashion surfboards. By today's standards, the boards were massive—about 9 feet long and 65 pounds.

Duke gave a board to 16-year-old Claude West, launching him as a future national champion for a decade.

The board survived pounding on rocks and falling off a truck. In 1956 West donated it to the Freshwater Surf Life Saving Club. The Clubhouse

Duke could have sold his boards before he left Australia and made a handsome profit. Some were apparently raffled for the war effort. With his typical aloha, he gave this board to teen Claude West, who became a legendary surfer. West later demonstrated the effectiveness of boards in rescues. West, shown here in 1975, is memorialized in an annual Long Board Classic Race, for 9-foot and 8-foot boards for men and women, at Manly, just south of Freshwater Beach.

COURTESY MANLY DAILY

burned down the next year. Alf Henderson, a Freshwater oldtimer, said the fire was so intense electric wiring melted and only a skeleton of the building remained. But the board survived.

It is now insured for $1 million and is a surfer's shrine. It may be the world's most expensive—and most loved—board.

◆

Duke returned twice to Freshwater. In 1956, he was an official guest at the Melbourne Olympics and head of Hawai'i's Territorial Delegation of swimmers, and once again he thrilled his fans by taking his board out into the surf. His last visit was in 1963 to visit his Freshwater 'ohana.

COURTESY FRESHWATER SURF LIFE SAVING CLUB

By 1956, Duke had many friends in Australia. Sadly, Sir Frank Beaurepaire, Lord Mayor of Melbourne, a fellow Olympian (who made a fortune from his appropriately named Olympic Tyre and Rubber Company), died weeks before Duke's arrival.

Freshwater honored Duke with a statue depicting him as a young man riding the pine board he fashioned with an adze on the beach in 1914. The statue stands high on a boulder on a windswept headland with sweeping views of the fine surfing beaches. It is visible for miles.

At dusk, automatic lights softly illuminate the bronze statue, increasing in intensity with the darkness. Duke comes alive, shining like a suntanned surfer. The huge honeycombed boulder is now a giant wave he is riding.

It is a "chickenskin" experience.

The dramatic statue of Duke on a huge boulder with the Pacific Ocean as its backdrop at Freshwater's Duke Kahanamoku Statue and Commemorative Park. Nadine dedicated the park January 26, 1994, and spoke of Duke's great love for Australia. Nadine herself is half Australian. Her late mother, opera singer Olive Kerr, was born in Adelaide.

The statue and park are a gift to the community from the Harbord Diggers Memorial Club (a war veterans/community club), the Warringah Shire Council, and the Freshwater Surf Life Saving Club.

A path of blonde Sydney sandstone meanders from the statue through the Duke Kahanamoku Commemorative Park, past a plaque honoring Duke, past two huge mosaic artworks highlighting his life.

Along the path, other stylized mosaic artworks honor Duke's inspiring Australian surfing legacy, one for each of the two dozen world champion surfers from the neighboring beaches—more world champions than the rest of the world combined. Australia has the highest rate of surfing participation in the world, one of every five males, one of every ten females.

◆

On January 26, 1994—Australia Day no less, because Australia claims him too—his name was the first inscribed on the surfing path in the Duke Kahanamoku Commemorative Park.

Eighty years after Duke's trip Down Under, Australian history books make scant reference to the real purpose of his visit. Even though he set countless records, including world records, even though he was the first foreign Olympian of any sport to visit, and even though the national meets were named the Kahanamoku Carnivals in his honor, what everyone remembers is his surfing.

COURTESY HARBORD DIGGERS MEMORIAL CLUB

Nadine Kahanamoku enjoys the dedication ceremonies for Duke's statue at Freshwater. With Nadine is Diggers Club's Malcolm "Mackie" Campbell, who worked for decades to see the statue become a reality.

"Duke shook my hand. I took it as my own personal invitation to Hawai'i," said Tom Blake.

William Blake, half-brother of surfing pioneer Tom Blake, remembers that Tom's life changed because of that handshake. Eighteen-year-old Blake, living in Wisconsin, was an unlikely person to become a famous swimmer and surfer. His life changed when he went to see a newsreel featuring the Antwerp Olympics. Standing in the Detroit theater lobby was Duke, the world champion.

Blake asked to shake his hand. "He held out his big, soft paw, and gave me a firm, hearty handshake."

Blake moved to Los Angeles, took up swimming and surfing, worked as a lifeguard. Later, he lived in Hawai'i for 25 years, as part of Duke's 'ohana.

Blake wrote in his 1935 book *Hawaiian Surfriders*, "To see Duke coming in at Waikiki on his long *olo* board was to see surfriding at its best. Somehow, to me, the Duke is the last of the Great Hawaiians, the man by which to measure the race, the surfrider by which to measure the surfriders of all time."

MID-PACIFIC MAGAZINE, JANUARY 1911

This photograph accompanied an article, "Riding the Surfboard," that Duke and other Hui Nalu members wrote for the first issue of the Mid-Pacific Magazine. *Its editor, Alexander Hume Ford, was determined to preserve the art and sport of surfing. He founded the Outrigger Canoe Club, the Trail and Mountain Club, and the Hands-Around-the-Pacific Club and also had ties to Mid-Pacific Institute. This wonderful photograph was used by the Australian sculptor of Duke's statue to determine Duke's foot placement.*

PHOTO BY A.R. GURREY, JR., COURTESY BISHOP MUSEUM

One of the few existing photographs of Duke riding tandem at Waikīkī. It was thrilling for the participants and spectators alike.

MID-PACIFIC MAGAZINE, JANUARY 1911

Duke had a repertoire of stunts, including jumping from one board to another and standing on his head (shown here).

"**Y**ou don't remember me, but I remember what you did for me . . . "

So began many letters sent when the news was flashed worldwide in December 1955 that Duke was hospitalized for a serious cardiac condition.

A Mr. Ralph Chambers wrote that when he was a homesick young soldier, stationed at Schofield Barracks 35 years before, Duke had expressed his aloha by teaching him, a stranger, how to surf.

"You probably don't remember me. I was having a hard time with my surfboard at Waikīkī. You came up and spent 30 minutes with me [and showed me what I was doing wrong]. Only later I found out who you were when someone called your name. I never got to thank you."

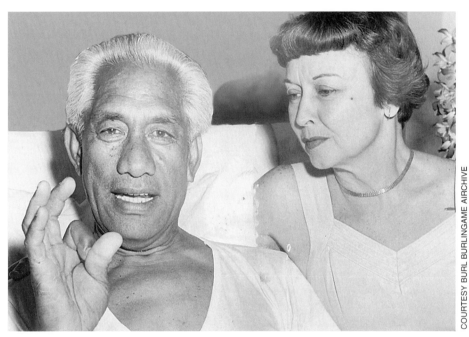

Duke enjoyed good health until his later years, except for a couple of bouts of influenza and some ear infections. In his 60s, he coped with a variety of ailments. Here, Nadine at his side, he recuperates from a cardiac condition. He left the hospital the next day after a 6-day stay. He accepted his health challenges philosophically. His only complaint was that his bed was 3 to 4 inches too short.

"**W**e hosted the West Coast Surfing Championships at Huntington Beach [California] in 1962. There must have been 10,000 kids on the beach, all kinds of little gremmies, and when Duke stepped out of the car it was like God had arrived. I couldn't believe the adulation," says Kimo Wilder McVay, Duke's personal manager for the last seven years of Duke's life. "It was two generations away from his prime; how could they know who he is? Surfing wasn't even that big then; surfers were like bums. That's when I was inspired to put together the Duke Kahanamoku Surfing Classic in Hawai'i. We elevated surfing through Duke in one fell swoop."

Q: "Do you have any tips you'd like to pass along to young surfers?"

Duke: "I think we have to teach a lot of these kids to first be gentlemen . . . . Try to help one another and not hog the doggone waves.

"You know, there are so many waves coming in all the time, you don't have to worry about that. Just take your time—wave comes. Let the other guys go; catch another one.

"And that's what we used to do. We'd see some other fella there first, and we'd say, 'You're here first. You take the first wave.'"

(*Surfer*, March 1965, pp. 29-33)

◆

"I used to surf Public Baths [surf break] when I was a small kid, and I was a hotshot out there," says Waikīkī beachboy and surfing great Rabbit Kekai. "Publics was our home ground. When it got big, Duke and them came down with their 16-foot boards, and us guys on our 5- and 6-foot boards with no skegs. We used to fly on those things. We used to watch Duke and those guys, he would be tracking down and flying on those 16-foot boards. We would never drop in on Duke when he was flying along, but we'd drop in on the other guys.

"For the Duke, there was respect. He got anything he wanted. No matter what spot he surfed, he got respect."

COURTESY BISHOP MUSEUM

Castle High and Intermediate School 8th graders and Duke at Bishop Museum. Duke came from a close, loving and supportive family, and he did what he could to encourage young people to set goals in life and achieve them. Notice how he has solved one boy's dilemma as to what to do with his hands. Duke has a no-nonsense hold on him.

Tom Blake, author, with Duke's input, of the first major account of Hawaiian surfing, made the first hollow longboard and pioneered surf-sailing, a predecessor to windsurfing.

He and Duke were a great team. Duke taught him the traditional ways of making and shaping boards; Blake studied, experimented, and made adaptations.

◆

In an August 23, 1965, *Honolulu Star-Bulletin* interview, Duke reflected, "The boards the kids are using today are okay but they're too light for me. My board was 16 feet of Californian redwood. I made it myself at Waikīkī without calipers to shape it.

"I would just feel it and say, need a little off here, that's pretty good, little bit here, and so on, until it was like I wanted it.

"Then I'd try it in the water after putting two coats of shellac on it. Finally it was just right. I took it out and caught a wave. I could feel it through my feet. I said, Oops, this is it Duke. Don't mess with it any more."

The *olo* board weighed 126 pounds. With no skeg, it was ideal for riding long distances. It was his favorite board for more than 20 years.

COURTESY HONOLULU STAR-BULLETIN

There are many fine collections of boards in Hawai'i, including those at the Hawai'i Maritime Center, Duke's Canoe Club and Restaurant, and the Bishop Museum. Duke is shown in 1957 with High Chief Abner Paki's koa boards. They weighed about 150 pounds. Paki is reputed to have ridden only waves deemed unsafe for others. Duke, like his father before him, was born at Paki's downtown Honolulu estate.

Tom Blake, the second person after Duke to be inducted into both the Swimming and Surfing Halls of Fame, reminisced in H. Arthur Klein's *Surf's Up!* (1966) about their days of surfing together:

"I would say that Duke attained his greatest surfing satisfactions and some of his greatest achievements as a rider after his fortieth year.

"It took a real man to carry Duke's new 126-pound board across the sand, and then into and out of the surf. It was even heavy in the water, responding slowly to a rider's efforts to turn and trim it. I tried it out, but I lacked the body weight to control it on a wave.

"However, Duke weighed about 210 pounds and it . . . seemed just right. And the board seemed suited to him in every way. The test came when we went out together on the first good day of storm surf at Waikīkī.

"Duke caught a big wave, then rose to his feet on the giant board. He was like a man transformed! The success of this ride went to his head like wine. He yelled and shouted at the top of his voice as he rode, sliding left on a big storm wave well outside the Cunha surfing area."

◆

In H. Arthur Klein's *Surf's Up!* (1966), Tom Blake remembers . . ."After completing his ride, Duke pulled and paddled back to join me.

"'Fine riding,' I said to him.

"'We're making history today,' was his answer.

"'What break do you call this?' I asked.

"'It's got no name—but let's give it one,' answered Duke.

"We were both riding our new long boards that we had made, so I suggested naming the break in [their] honor. I asked Duke what the Hawaiian word was for the big boards like [ours].

"'Papa nui,' was Duke's reply. *Papa* stands for 'board,' and *nui* for 'big.' . . . In all the years since that memorable day in 1932, hundreds of surfers have talked about . . . the Papa Nui break . . . , but no one has ever questioned the origin of the name."

In H. Arthur Klein's *Surf's Up!* (1966), Tom Blake remembers Duke as the greatest longboard surfer at Waikīkī:

"In 1932, the Duke did some of the most beautiful riding I have ever seen on his new long board. In one instance at Zero Break he caught a 25-foot wave, and rode across the face of it, through First Break, clear into Queen's Surf, at a speed of about thirty miles an hour, for a ride of about four hundred yards.

"Duke can catch the wave one hundred yards farther out than the boys with the short . . . boards."

Duke poses effortlessly with another of his longboards in 1934. Note the width of the board. It would take great shoulder and arm strength to paddle this board, lying prone or kneeling.

One of Eugenia "Genie" McMahon's most poignant memories is the elderly Duke asking John, her late husband, "Do me a favor. Take my longboard out. Catch a few waves. It's been landlocked too long. Needs to get wet."

"While Duke sat watching at the Outrigger with his rheumy eyes, John wove and slid across Duke's waves, on Duke's board, for Duke.

"Typical Duke, he said nothing, just sat, alone with his thoughts. Words were unnecessary."

◆

"He had a way of imparting wisdom to me without ever being condescending," says former world champion surfer and Hawai'i state legislator Fred Hemmings. "One day I asked him, 'Duke, how did you ever get that legendary ride from Outside Castles to the Moana?' He said, 'Freddie, no one could make that ride today.'

"I was taken aback, because it sounded like he was bragging. But then he went on to explain. 'When I got that ride it was before they built the Ala Wai Canal and at that time all the streams emptied into Waikīkī.' So basically there was a logical, scientific reason for what he claimed. The bottom had changed so much since they closed the streams that the waves didn't line up any more to allow that kind of magnificent ride. This was the kind of basic awareness and wisdom that Duke had. No one will ever accuse him of being a very scholarly person, but he was a very wise person."

Duke relaxing at the old Outrigger Canoe Club with fellow member and surfer John McMahon. The photo was taken about 1963, when Duke was in his early 70s.

COURTESY EUGENIA MCMAHON

PAUL STRAUCH, JR.   JOEY CABELL   THE DUKE   FRED HEMMINGS

BUTCH VAN ARTSDALEN

Members of Duke Kahanamoku's Surf Team traveled across the United States giving demonstrations. The team is posed in 1965 with new, lightweight boards bearing Duke's name. They were sold in major stores such as Sears and J.C. Penney before the advent of surfing specialty shops.

Like any other surfer, Duke sustained the occasional bump on the head, bruise or scrape.

Q. "What was your worst wipeout, Duke?"

Duke: "Outside the Natatorium. The waves were big that day—about 25 feet I'd guess. And they were coming fast—one right after the other—and I got caught [in the waves]. I thought, the only way I can save myself is not to struggle—not to fight the wave and just—[be calm] . . . . Just sit and wait for the waves as they come in. Then [when] they hit you, just hold your breath . . . and go under five or six feet where it's not so [turbulent]. Well, these waves were coming so fast, I was almost ready to call for help.

"I said, 'Hang on, and pray. God will help me and keep me afloat and then I'll be all right.' And that's what happened."

(*Surfer,* March 1965, pp. 29-33)

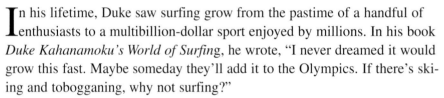

In his lifetime, Duke saw surfing grow from the pastime of a handful of enthusiasts to a multibillion-dollar sport enjoyed by millions. In his book *Duke Kahanamoku's World of Surfing,* he wrote, "I never dreamed it would grow this fast. Maybe someday they'll add it to the Olympics. If there's skiing and tobogganing, why not surfing?"

The Olympics of 2000 will be hosted by Sydney, Australia. It would be fitting if his lifetime dream is realized there.

When Duke was a teenager, there were few surfers in the whole world. Many times, he said, there were only a handful of surfers at Waikīkī.

By the end of his life, anywhere there were waves, there were surfers. If there was no ocean, no problem. Waves were created by wave machines, in landlocked places like Arizona.

Fifty million people watched the televised Sunset Beach first annual Duke Kahanamoku Invitational Surfing Championships in 1965. It was nominated for an Emmy for the best sports production of the year.

Yet the man known as the International Father of Modern Surfing never won a major surfing championship, never won money from it. He surfed for the love of it.

When the Huntington Surfing Walk of Fame was created in 1994 to honor surfing greats, the first name—requiring no vote—was Duke's.

PHOTO BY RICK REIF

Duke's was the first tile laid in the sidewalk Surfing Walk of Fame, at the corner of Main Street and Pacific Coast Highway, Huntington Beach, California. Duke was also the only one selected without being put to a vote, as there was only one Father of Surfing. For the other categories, nominations were solicited from surf-affliliated voters worldwide, with about 40 nominees in each category. Selected were Joyce Hoffman, Tom Blake, Mark Richards, Bruce Brown, and Robert August.

Ali'i

Although Duke was not a duke, he was a descendant of
Hawaiian royalty, and his achievements in swimming and
surfing, along with his good looks and unaffected charm,
brought him the attention and admiration of royalty and a
nine-year career in Hollywood. Whether rescuing people at
sea or serving as Hawai'i's official Ambassador of Aloha, he
was always gracious, never capitalizing on his fame.

Twenty-year-old Mickey Rooney, one of Hollywood's most popular film stars, is sworn in as an honorary deputy sheriff on his arrival in March 1941. Hawai'i was fortunate to have such a famous and photogenic person as Duke to willingly pose for this type of photograph. The tourist industry benefited with millions of dollars of free publicity—especially when these photos of Paradise ran during the mainland winter.

"He won his gold medals in the Olympics in 1912 [and 1920]," says Kimo Wilder McVay, Duke's personal manager for the last seven years of Duke's life. "There was no television, just radio and newspapers, and he caught the imagination of everyone. He put Hawai'i on the map; no one had ever heard of this Hawai'i before then. . . .

"He was so colorful, such a hero, just exactly what everyone expected a gold medalist Olympic champion to look like. He was Hawai'i, wherever he went, across the U.S. and around the world.

"He was on a first-name basis with celebrities all over the world. He was a celebrity's celebrity. For years and years, anybody who had any knowledge of sports knew about Duke in the Olympics. At that time surfing was nothing. He had no fame from the movies, because he just played bit parts. . . . But to celebrities, he was their hero. . . .

"It was fun to set up things and watch people react to them, because he was such a magnificent-looking guy. He looked like a king.

"From a standpoint of fame, you couldn't ask for a better role model as far as a good, decent human being, a kind human being who shared whatever he had with everyone else. . . . Everyone was his friend."

———————————◆———————————

Many people thought "Duke" was a title, but it was a name, derived from a title, that came about this way:

There was great excitement in Honolulu on July 21, 1869, when Alfred, second in line to the British throne, arrived in Honolulu on a goodwill visit. He was a guest of High Chief Abner Paki, descendant of the Kamehamehas. Living at Paki's estate, Haleakalā, in downtown Honolulu, were the *kahus'* families, the Chief's trusted retainers and advisers. The Kahanamokus had long been *kahus* of the Kamehamehas, since their days together on the Big Island. On the day of Alfred's arrival, a son was born at Haleakalā to the Kahanamokus. A custom that perpetuates is to invite a *kupuna* or *ali'i* to select a suitable name for a newborn baby.

Paki's daughter, Bernice Pauahi Paki (Bishop), chose the name "Duke," in honor of the young Duke of Edinburgh's visit, and to imbue the babe with the qualities of Queen Victoria's family, whom she greatly admired. The baby's full name was Duke Halapu Kahanamoku—and 21 years later, he would be Duke Paoa Kahanamoku's father.

(Pukui, Elbert, and Mookini, *Place Names of Hawaii,* 1974, p. 63)

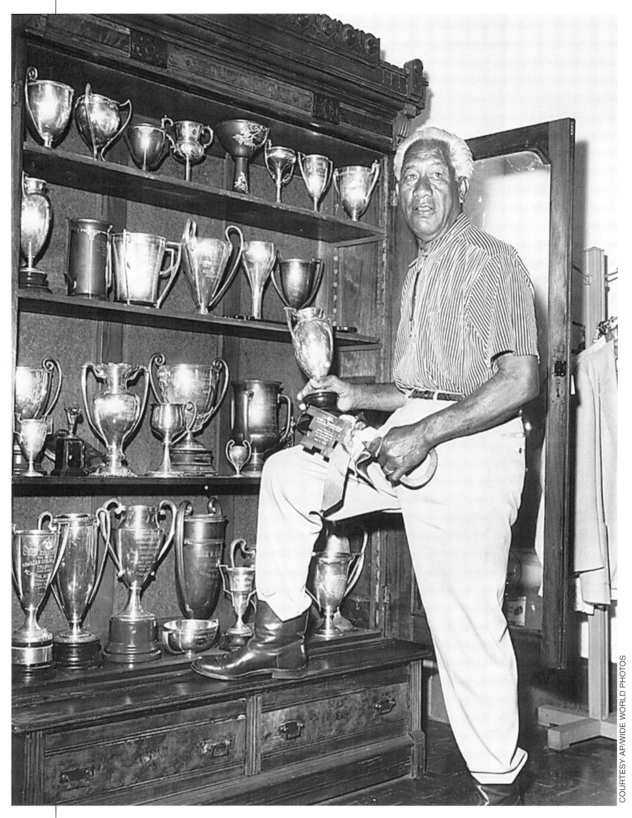

Duke won thousands of trophies, each one a symbol of not just victory, but of sportsmanship and respect for his fellow competitors. He embodied what Baron de Coubertin, founder of the modern Olympics, said: "The important thing in the Olympic Games is not winning, but taking part. The essential thing in life is not conquering, but fighting well."

Gertrude "Gee" Lawrence, one of the English-speaking world's most famous actresses, was touring the Pacific in 1945 for the United Service Organizations (USO). Her husband, Richard Stoddard Aldrich, in his 1954 biography *Gertrude Lawrence as Mrs. A.: An Intimate Biography of the Great Star,* describes his wife's confusion over Duke's name: When she arrived in Honolulu, she told her host that she wanted to see "one of my very good friends, Nadine Alexander, [who] is married to a Polynesian nobleman, the Duke of Kahanamoku."

She instructed the telephone operator to connect her to the residence of the Duke of Kahanamoku. Gee asked for "Her Grace, the Duchess of Kahanamoku." She was told, "Mrs. Kahanamoku is out, but will call back."

Nadine later explained, "Gee, I'm sorry to disappoint you, but though my husband does have royal blood, I'm just plain Mrs. Kahanamoku of O'ahu, just as you are Mrs. Aldrich of Cape Cod."

PHOTO BY LEROY GRANNIS

A glamorous Nadine in early 1965. Although she may not be "Duchess" by title, she has always had the bearing of an aristocrat.

In his *Honolulu Advertiser* column of May 4, 1967, Eddie Sherman told of Gabi Otten, a 9-year-old West German girl who addressed a letter to "The Duke of Honolulu Kahanamoku, South Seas."

Addressing him as "Your Highness," Gabi requested some of his "homeland's stamps."

COURTESY EDDIE SHERMAN

Eddie Sherman and Duke attended the opening of a new Sheraton in Texas. Sherman, a veteran newspaper columnist, has forgotten the date and the name of the hotel, but he will never forget the great excitement at the reception when Duke's presence was announced.

Before Britain's Queen Elizabeth, the Queen Mother, arrived in Honolulu, officials discussed protocol, including who should place a lei on her royal shoulders.

Duke joked that he should. He was closest to royalty of anyone in Hawai'i; he had met the past and future kings of Sweden, King Leopold and his sons the Princes Alfred and Baudouin of Belgium, plus the British Prince of Wales, Lord Mountbatten and many others.

The Queen Mum was enchanted by Duke, and performed a spontaneous hula with him at the airport.

PHOTO BY WERNER STOY, CAMERA HAWAII, COURTESY BISHOP MUSEUM

Queen Elizabeth, the British Queen Mother, flying from Australia to London, landed for a brief stop in Honolulu. Greeted with Hawaiian music, she told Gov. John A. Burns that she felt like dancing. Burns summoned Duke, and the 65-year-old Queen Mum imitated Duke's movements. As she danced, she asked Nadine how she was doing. Once again, Nadine became a dance instructor, telling the Queen to raise her hands, just as this memorable photograph, which appeared on newspaper front pages worldwide, was snapped. Yes, that is a hat the Queen is wearing—made of white ostrich feathers.

Many songs and hulas were written about Duke. There was the "Duke Kahanamoku, Former Olympic Champion, Now Pumping Gas" song, songs by Sol Bright, Gene Burdette, and others. Duke himself sang on several records and in the movies. With Waltah Clarke's group, he led the singing of "Aloha 'Oe," and he sang in the 1930 movie *Isle of Escape*.

Songwriter Hank Fort composed a song as a special Christmas present in 1962. Fort met Duke and Nadine on Christmas Eve. Fort phoned Duke next day, said "Mele Kalīkimaka," and crooned:

"The Prince of Royalty is Duke Kahanamoku of Hawai'i.
If you visit this island, this magic land,
You learn the legend and you understand
Why he's the prince of royalty, Duke Kahanamoku of Hawai'i.
Everywhere he goes, everybody knows him well, and loves to tell
That it's all because of him the *humuhumunukunukuāpua'a* can swim.
So strum your uke and sing to the Duke who's king
Of the islands of Old Hawai'i."

(*Honolulu Advertiser*, January 9, 1963)

COURTESY BISHOP MUSEUM

Prince Edward Albert, later the Duke of Windsor, visited in April 1920 for the Hawaiian Missions' Centennial. A good sport, he allowed the beachboys to call him Kawika, which is Hawaiian for David, his familial name. Some of his aides were not too happy at this informality; nor were they amused when the then-future King of England fell off his surfboard and disappeared for a few anxious moments. He had such a good time he made an unscheduled return visit.

COURTESY HONOLULU STAR-BULLETIN

The East Coast press decided that Duke's large feet and his novel flutter kick were what gave him a competitive edge. Cartoonists frequently exaggerated the size of his feet.

Duke insured his feet for $50,000 with Lloyds' Insurance Company of London in 1918, before leaving on a 30-city tour to raise money for the Liberty Bond War effort. The news account reported that Willie Hoppe, the pool player, and Ignatz Paderewski, the pianist, insured their hands, but Duke insured his "pedals."

Duke had hands that were bigger than average—all the better to paddle a canoe with; feet that were bigger than average—all the better to propel him across the water; and his doctor said he had a heart twice as big as normal. But everyone who knew him knew his heart was much bigger than that.

◆

"He was concerned about everybody, especially the guys who were working the beach. He knew it wasn't easy, that you had to have a special type of talent," says former Waikīkī beachboy George Downing.

"He was really a wonderful host; he went out of his way to extend himself to people. When he took people out in a canoe, he had a sensitivity to the guy who was a little older and didn't necessarily know how to handle himself getting in and out of the canoe. His hand was always at the right place, without having to make a big thing out of it. He always had a shoulder there and an arm there to lean on to maintain the individual's self-respect.

"And yet the strength of this man was remarkable. His small finger was as big as my thumb. He was powerful and gentle."

Movie actor/director Douglas Fairbanks, Sr., and his second wife, Mary Pickford, "discovered" Duke and encouraged him to pursue a movie career. Fairbanks, one of the most popular actors of his time, was himself a fine athlete. He appreciated Duke's abilities and saw Duke's potential. However, he was unaware of the intricacies of the issues of amateurism versus professionalism.

During his almost 10 years in Hollywood, Duke appeared in about 30 movies. It is to Duke's credit that he managed as many roles as he did, although some were very minor, and some quite forgettable. Duke's career also bridged the old silent movies and the "talkies." By nature, he was more suited to the silent movies.

His manager, Dr. Oscar Henning, worked hard to get suitable roles for Duke, but he was faced with two problems. Duke could not get paid for swimming in movies—which is what the public wanted to see. The Amateur Athletic Union was unrealistic and rigid about their definition of "amateur." Duke did not want to jeopardize any future national and Olympic participation. The second problem was casting. Directors had very narrow and stereotypical ideas of what was an appropriate role for a brown-skinned man.

COURTESY THE ACADEMY OF MOTION PICTURE ARTS AND SCIENCES

Duke in the 1925 silent movie Lord Jim, *based on Joseph Conrad's great sea novel. Duke played a faithful servant to Percy Marmont (left) in the title role. The movie was directed by Victor Fleming, who became famous for directing* The Wizard of Oz *and most of* Gone with the Wind.

Englishman Ronald Colman was a movie idol from the 1920s until his death in 1958. He personified the aristocracy. His beautiful speaking voice helped him make a successful transition from silent movies to sound. He was unforgettable as Sydney Carton in Tale of Two Cities. *Duke appeared with him in a small part in* The Rescue *in 1929. Duke is wearing a famous sweatshirt (its whereabouts currently unknown) signed by his fellow film actors.*

COURTESY BURL BURLINGAME AIRCHIVE

COURTESY THE ACADEMY OF MOTION PICTURE ARTS AND SCIENCES

The most beloved star of the silent screen, Douglas Fairbanks, Sr., with his agility and devil-may-care attitude, was the prototype of the American male. He admired Duke very much, and they often played golf together. Fairbanks made good on a 1929 promise to return to Hawai'i, returning in 1931 to co-direct Around the World in Eighty Minutes, *a film diary with stops in Hawai'i, Japan, China, and other parts of Asia. In the film, Duke rode a board at Waikiki, one of the few times he was seen surfing on the big screen.*

Duke was a lifelong advocate of lifesaving and learn-to-swim programs. He was always hauling half-drowned swimmers out of the water. It would be impossible to count the number of lives he saved.

In 1925 he was proclaimed a national hero for rescuing 8 drowning fishermen at Newport Beach, California. According to the April 18, 1953, *Honolulu Star-Bulletin*, Newport Police Chief Porter said, "The Duke's performance was the most superhuman rescue act and the finest display of surfboard riding that has ever been seen in the world, I believe."

The *Thelma,* a 40-foot, 5-ton yacht with 17 fishing buddies aboard, capsized in heavy seas in the notoriously unpredictable Newport breakwater. A large wave smashed the engine-room hatch, disabling the engine. Everyone was swept overboard. Some of the fishermen, knocked unconscious, never had a chance. When another wave tore off part of the rigging, the boat capsized.

The 35-year-old Duke, with Los Angeles Athletic Club (LAAC) friends Gerard Vultee and Owen Hale, leapt on their longboards and headed out to the flailing men. Duke paddled out and back 3 times through heavy seas. The 8 he rescued were semiconscious or injured. Hale and Vultee rescued another 4. The 3 exhausted surfers later retrieved 5 bodies.

The police chief said, "Many more would have drowned, but for the quick action of the Hawaiian swimmer."

When asked how he managed to rescue so many, Duke had very little to say, "I do not know. It was done. That is the main thing. By a few tricks, perhaps." He was devastated that so many drowned.

Duke, Owen Hale, and Gerard Vultee were honored for rescuing 12 drowning fishermen. Hale (center) was one of California's champion swimmers in 1913, and both he and Vultee were pioneer surfers.

COURTESY LOS ANGELES ATHLETIC CLUB

In the fall, his heroism was acknowledged by the Hawaiian Society of Los Angeles at a gala reception, and the LAAC honored its 3 heroes with gold watches on Christmas Day 1925.

Thirty-two years later, 3 of the grateful men whose lives he saved thanked him in person before a national television audience on NBC's *This Is Your Life*. Duke still did not have much to say. He simply said, "That's okay."

COURTESY BURL BURLINGAME AIRCHIVE

Duke, shown here with Ralph Edwards, thought he was doing a television promotion for Hawai'i in 1957 when he walked onto an NBC sound stage simulating Waikīkī Beach. He was surprised, and moved to tears, to discover that he was the subject of This Is Your Life. *Nadine, who had helped plan it, was there, as were all his brothers and sisters, "Dad" Center, F. Lang Akana (his longtime deputy sheriff), and three* Thelma *survivors. He was reunited with former Olympians Johnny Weissmuller, "Ludy" Langer, Michael McDermott, and many other friends.*

Duke got to know hundreds of movie stars. He knew Charlie Chaplin well—Chaplin lived at the LAAC. Dean Martin, Kirk Douglas, Clark Gable, Wallace Beery, Vincent Price, Cyd Charisse, Debbie Reynolds, Tony Martin—their names would fill pages.

COURTESY HAWAI'I MARITIME CENTER

Duke clowns with Groucho Marx on Marx's visit to Hawai'i. During Duke's years in Hollywood, he met many actors at the Hollywood Athletic Club, Los Angeles Athletic Club, or Santa Monica Beach Club, where he was a lifeguard. Duke apparently knew everyone, and everyone knew Duke. LAAC members included Frank Baum (Wizard of Oz), Rudolph Valentino, Will Rogers, Jr., the Los Angeles Times *Chandlers and many others.*

Ten years old and already a veteran, Shirley Temple arrived on the S.S. Matsonia *with her mother (behind Duke) in May 1939—her third visit to Hawai'i. Wherever she went, she was mobbed by fans anxious to see her, touch her, and perhaps present her with a lei. Sheriff Duke provided a calm, strong presence.*

Duke was on hand to greet Charlie Chaplin and Paulette Goddard, star of Chaplin's Modern Times, *who were through passengers, via Honolulu, returning from a four-month tour in Asia. Anticipating reporters' questions, Chaplin blew a big cloud of smoke, waddled a little, and started the interview by announcing, "I am neither dead, married, retired, lost, strayed, stolen, nor about to become any of the same."* (Honolulu Advertiser, *May 30, 1936)*

Duke enjoyed starring with another Duke—John Wayne—in MGM's *Wake of the Red Witch*. (The ambiguous title refers to the wave left behind by the boat the *Red Witch*.) Wayne gave Duke a coffee mug with the inscription "to Duke from the Duke," which Kahanamoku thought was amusing.

Years later, when asked about his role, he said, "My part? A chief, what else! A pearl chief this time. I owned all the pearls in the Pacific (which is not bad). What would I do with all those pearls in real life? I'd be a pearl merchant. I'd go around the world selling one here, one there. Give a lot away.

"I've always wanted to go around the world. I've seen about half of it by now. I'd like to go to Japan and South America. Maybe drop down to Australia. I like to keep moving."

(*Honolulu Advertiser*, October 18, 1954)

COURTESY BURL BURLINGAME AIRCHIVE

Two of the world's most famous Dukes in The Wake of the Red Witch, *in 1948. This was Kahanamoku's first movie in 15 years. He finally was cast as a chief, rather than as a native boy, an Arab, a Turk, or even a Tripolitan. Left to right, director Edmund Granger, Duke, and John "Duke" Wayne.*

A still from The Wake of the Red Witch. *Chief Duke (center) is interrupted at his sumptuous luau by John Wayne. Notice the stock props, such as the idol.*

Even after Duke left Hollywood, his friends from his movie days sought him out in Hawai'i.

John Ford, the movie director, often visited Hawai'i in *Araner*, his 120-foot floating palace. Ford directed Duke in the award-winning 1955 movie *Mister Roberts*, starring Henry Fonda, James Cagney, William Powell, and Jack Lemmon. On several occasions, Duke—and later Nadine—stayed with the Fords at their California ranch.

Duke on board the Araner *with John Ford, one of Hollywood's most honored movie directors. Ford was a colorful character, as this photograph shows. He frequently visited Hawai'i, where he was very popular.*

COURTESY LIBRARY OF CONGRESS, PRINTS AND PHOTOGRAPHS DIVISION, NYWT & S COLLECTION

COURTESY LIBRARY OF CONGRESS, PRINTS AND PHOTOGRAPHS DIVISION, NYWT & S COLLECTION

Newlyweds Florence Rice and Robert Wilcox were "hitched" with a lei by Sheriff Duke. The bride's father was Grantland Rice, one of the most famous sports columnists of his time, who often wrote about Duke. Rice was unable to attend the wedding, so Duke stood in for him and gave the bride away. The March 1939 wedding took place on Coconut Island, Kāne'ohe Bay, at Christian R. Holmes's estate. The newlyweds were both movie stars.

The King: Elvis Presley. The Colonel: Tom Parker, Elvis's manager. The Duke. The three played important roles in raising money for the Pacific War Memorial Commission of Hawai'i. The goal: build a suitable memorial to honor the 1,177 officers and men entombed in the USS *Arizona* at Pearl Harbor on December 7, 1941.

Duke was a member of the blue-ribbon Commission, formed right after the war's end. The fund-raising bogged down after 15 years. The memorial received a boost when Elvis unexpectedly volunteered to perform in Hawai'i at a fund-raising concert.

The concert was a great success. Elvis donated over $50,000, which encouraged other donations, and the memorial was finally completed.

Colonel Tom Parker, Elvis Presley's ebullient manager, arrived in 1961 for his protégé's Hawai'i performance to raise money for the Arizona *Memorial at Pearl Harbor. That's Mrs. Parker flanked by Duke and the Colonel.*

COURTESY *HONOLULU STAR-BULLETIN*

A study in contrasts: Duke, reserved and private, Arthur Godfrey, the gregarious, most popular radio and television personality in the United States.

A close friend for more than 20 years, Godfrey arranged frequent guest appearances for Duke that helped to promote Hawai'i and Duke's line of merchandise—beach clothing and accessories, surfboards and so on.

Their correspondence shows Duke trusted Godfrey implicitly. He discussed everything with him—business, new ideas to promote Hawaiian tourism, health, family, and sailing. With Godfrey—whom he nicknamed "Mino'aka" (smiling one)—he showed his vulnerable side and his great sense of humor.

Arthur Godfrey
United States of America

Aloooooha MINO'AKA:

Mele Kalīkimaka ame Hau'oli Makahiki Hou iā 'oe a me kou 'ohana ā pau.
[Merry Christmas and Happy New Year to you and all your family.]

If Santa brought me nothing else than this most wonderful and inspirational letter from you, I feel that I have received more than my share of Christmas Aloha. Certainly I feel much closer to you now. Thank you very much for your sentiments, and I appreciate it very much.

Your friendship to me is something we Hawaiians would say in one word, *'ihi'ihi,* which means "sacred and treasured." I believe this mutual Aloha stems from the fact that we both had to learn the hard way. Having had the steeled experiences of life, we recognize real friendship when we meet it, and I want to again say, that I have long considered you as one of my real *"hoa-aloha pumehana."*

Following his signature, he added a little P.S.

If can, write some more.
If too busy, I wait.

(Excerpted from a Christmas 1952 letter)

Two years later, he wrote Mino'aka a short note of consolation. Godfrey was paying the price of celebrity—taking a beating in the press over something they both agreed was trivial. Duke's quiet strength comes through.

"I believe in you my friend. Keep your chin up and keep punching. They'll drop."

COURTESY BURL BURLINGAME AIRCHIVE

Arthur Godfrey and Duke first met in the 1940s when Godfrey was stationed in Hawai'i in the Navy. Duke helped him refine his banjo playing. Godfrey ruffled feathers on occasion—he once said that the State of Hawai'i woefully underpaid Duke as Ambassador of Aloha. This is true, of course, considering the multimillion-dollar contracts today's athletes receive for endorsements and the time and energy Duke spent promoting Hawai'i.

No U.S. President before Franklin Delano Roosevelt had ever visited Hawai'i while in office. He was met off the O'ahu coast by an escort of 100 planes. A flotilla of 14 canoes escorted his cruiser to the pier. Duke rode in a double-hulled canoe to greet him, dressed as Kamehameha. An estimated 60,000 people greeted Roosevelt.

Later, Duke was honored to take the President's two sons paddling and surfing. The boys, John and Franklin, Jr., enjoyed themselves so much they were reluctant to leave Hawai'i and begged their father to allow them to stay.

FDR's visit was a display of America's might and patriotism. Roosevelt's sons welcomed the opportunity to relax at Waikīkī with Duke, who taught them how to surf. Left to right, John, Duke, Franklin, Jr.

COURTESY HAWAII STATE ARCHIVES

In the late 1930s, Scripps-Howard war correspondent Ernie Pyle wrote: "At Waikīkī the tourists pester him. Always wanting to take his picture. He is by nature courteous and kind, and usually obliges. If you go up and introduce yourself, and ask if he minds letting you take his picture, he'll pose every time.

"But he says so many barge at him and yell: 'Hey you. Get up there. Want your picture.'

"To those people he says: 'I'm sorry. I'm not in the mood for a picture today.'

"Duke hasn't any money to speak of. Before his election he had some [gasoline] filling stations around Honolulu. Now he just has his Sheriff's salary, and a little change from royalties here and there. He is called upon to spend far more than he makes.

"Practically everybody here knows him. There is a constant stream of people hitting him for jobs, or favors, or a handout of a dollar or two. 'I just had to stop it,' he says 'I didn't have the money.'

"He has friends all over the world, and they're always cabling him to meet some friend of theirs at the boat. He has to spend his own money to be a sort of unofficial host for the islands.

"He has never capitalized on his fame. That's one reason why he's still poor—and also why Hawai'i regards him so highly. I suppose there isn't a man in Honolulu—white, brown or yellow—who wouldn't be proud to walk down the street with Duke Kahanamoku."

(Honolulu Advertiser, March 1938)

"I don't think I ever heard Duke speak of money. You know how people get into conversations about acquiring money or getting money for something you do," says former Waikīkī beachboy George Downing, who was usually putting his rental equipment away just as Duke arrived at the beach to relax after a day of work.

"He had his canoes and surfboards there at the Outrigger Canoe Club, so he'd come and work, patching his boards and canoes. He always took care of his equipment. He had such respect for it. It was like a ritual: he used it, he cleaned it, he took great care of it. He put his aloha into it.

"I could see he wanted to be alone, but people would come up to him, and his friendliness and courtesy were amazing. He would stop and acknowledge them. He always seemed to be this smiling, friendly guy. They would say, 'Hi Duke, remember me from Europe and the Olympics?' And he would always say, 'Yeah, I remember you.' I never ever saw him in a bad mood.

"I saw him at times when he needed to be by himself, and his sense of humor was tremendous; his memory was amazing.

"He had piercing eyes. You could tell if everything was OK, or there was a problem. He went about doing things very quietly to smooth things over, making sure there was harmony, to make sure things ran smoothly on the beach. If somebody got out of hand, he knew how to take care of it without being abrasive. That was something special. When anyone had a problem, they would say, 'Let's go to Duke. Duke will handle it.'

"He didn't have to say anything twice."

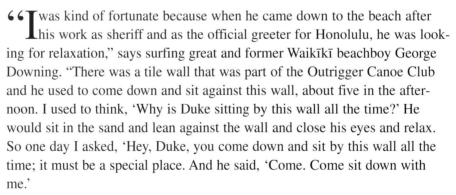

"I was kind of fortunate because when he came down to the beach after his work as sheriff and as the official greeter for Honolulu, he was looking for relaxation," says surfing great and former Waikīkī beachboy George Downing. "There was a tile wall that was part of the Outrigger Canoe Club and he used to come down and sit against this wall, about five in the afternoon. I used to think, 'Why is Duke sitting by this wall all the time?' He would sit in the sand and lean against the wall and close his eyes and relax. So one day I asked, 'Hey, Duke, you come down and sit by this wall all the time; it must be a special place. And he said, 'Come. Come sit down with me.'

"So I went back and sat with him, and he said, 'Lean back.' So I leaned back and, oh, I got it. He never said anything to me, but I got what it was. During the day the sun used to heat this wall up and in the late afternoon the heat was radiating from this wall. So when you put your back against it, oh man, the relief of this heat coming through the wall. He looked at me and smiled, and never said anything because he knew I got it. This is the kind of person he was; everything was mellow."

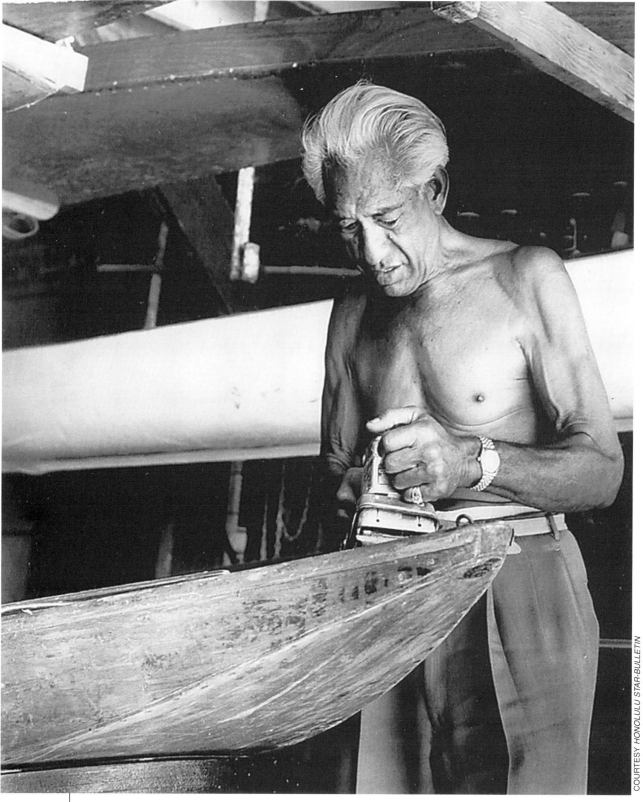

COURTESY HONOLULU STAR-BULLETIN

Duke was not materialistic or wasteful. He took good care of all his possessions. In this photograph in 1963, he uses an electric sander on his Australian surf ski, a gift to him in 1939 when a team of Australian surf lifesavers and swimmers came to compete in an aquatics meet. Knowing that Aussies enjoy a good laugh, then-Sheriff Duke staged a mock arrest and lock-up of the visiting officials.

Duke loved his wax look-alike. He would stop by and say "Hi, braddah!" Fred Jeckell, the museum's president and founder, said he and Duke had a standing routine. "Duke would take my hand, put it on his arm, and laugh and say, 'More bettah than wax, huh?' And we'd laugh some more."

Jeckell had been a fan of Duke's since seeing him swim in 1918 in Victoria, British Columbia.

The model, molded 2-1/2 years before his death, greeted tourists outside the Hawaiian Wax Museum on Kalākaua Avenue. Tourists loved posing with "Duke" to have their picture taken.

The model wore Duke's shoes and bolo tie. The old *koa* wood paddle and the redwood board were two of his most treasured possessions. After Duke's death, the wax "braddah" was replaced by a wax model of Don Ho. After the museum closed, the wax model was discarded.

(*Honolulu Star-Bulletin and Advertiser*, January 19, 1969)

COURTESY *HONOLULU STAR-BULLETIN*

The Wax Museum in the heart of Waikīkī attracted over 120,000 visitors a year, and it was a vacation tradition to pose with the lifelike model of Duke. If visitors were fortunate, they might see the real Duke himself at his restaurant.

An identical wax figure was erected at the International Swimming Hall of Fame in Florida. Mrs. E. "Ma" Fullard-Leo, one of the driving forces behind the Hawaiian branch of the Amateur Athletic Union, donated lava rocks from Mauna Loa to make a backdrop.

The wax models from the Hawai'i museum are long gone, but, fortunately, duplicates have been kept at the International Swimming Hall of Fame in Florida. More than 300,000 visitors each year see the replicas of Duke and his friend Johnny Weissmuller.

Toward the end of his life, Duke drove luxury cars—a bright-red Lincoln Continental and a Rolls Royce, courtesy of the restaurant that bore his name.

James Pflueger of Pflueger Motors gave him a vanity license plate in 1963, years before they were permitted. Technically, he was breaking the law, as the law stated that both front and rear plates had to be visible.

In the 1930s a special 8-inch, gold-plated hood ornament of a surfer was crafted for the Duke. It was a labor of love by the artist parents of surfer-environmentalist John Kelly. His father posed for the upper portion of the statue, and young John posed for the legs, as he was a surfer and got the stance just right by posing on a surfboard in their Black Point backyard.

On New Year's Eve, 1965, the hood ornament was stolen from Duke's car. Curiously, five months later, two young children presented him with a silver-plated replica. The original was discovered in Modesto, California, and eventually returned to him.

Duke had several different car hood ornaments, made out of trophies or created especially for him by friends. He was very trusting and was shocked when this gold-plated ornament was stolen.

COURTESY FRED HEMMINGS

On a promotional tour of Southern California shopping centers, the Father of International Modern Surfing is stoked, standing next to his Rolls Royce, with surfboards, accompanied by convivial friends (left to right, Fred Hemmings Jr., Paul Strauch, Jr., and Butch Van Artsdalen). At 76, Duke looks as though he is enjoying himself every bit as much as in his Olympic years.

"Back when Duke Kahanamoku's Restaurant was new, Kimo McVay had just made Don Ho a star," says former world champion surfer and Hawai'i state legislator Fred Hemmings.

"Don had just gone from Honey's [in Kane'ohe] to Duke's Restaurant, and in 1966 he was heading for his first mainland gig at the Ambassador Hotel's Cocoanut Grove [in Los Angeles]. It had headlined some major stars, and Don Ho opened to a record-breaking act there.

"At that time we had formed the Duke Kahanamoku Surf Team in the early '60s to promote a Duke line of clothing and other things, and Kimo McVay had arranged a surfing trip with us to go down to Malibu in a Rolls Royce. So we put the boards on the top and took some pictures. We got down to Malibu, and Duke, who was 76, said 'OK, boys, I'll stay in the car and you go surf.'

"We had all been at the Don Ho performance all night, and every night was like a party. So Duke went to sleep in the car.

"After about an hour and a half of surfing I noticed a crowd on the beach and I said to myself, 'Oh no, don't tell me there's a beef or a fight or something.' And there was a bunch of Malibu guys and of course fellow club members from Hawai'i Paul Strauch and Butch Van Artsdalen and a young lady, very attractive, I might say.

"She might have been consuming illegal substances and was gyrating around totally nude and having a good time. Of course, the surfers were loving it.

"Pretty soon the police arrived and were coming down the hill and right behind them was Duke. He said, 'What's going on?' And we told him, 'Ah, you missed it.' And he said, 'Hey, you boys, next time wake me up.'

"Here's this 76-year-old guy who still had an eye for a fun time. That's what kind of guy he was. I think his lifelong relationship with the ocean kept him young and served him well."

Another name besides Duke's that conjures up visions of Hawai'i is that of charismatic popular singer Don Ho. With a repertoire of over 300 songs, Don and the Ali'is never had a set show; things just evolved, with audience participation in jokes, sing-alongs, and solos. One trademark song, featured on the glassware at Duke Kahanamoku's Restaurant, was "Suck 'em Up."

In a letter to the editor appearing in the April 14, 1967, *Honolulu Star-Bulletin*, a woman wrote

"My husband and I had one of the most thrilling and memorable experiences of our two-year military tour here. As Duke Kahanamoku came out of a store on Kapiʻolani Blvd., I hesitated at first to even bother him knowing of his recent hospitalization. I asked if he would pose in front of his car for us for a photograph. Not only did he do this, but he suggested we take it in turns to pose with him! He has such an interesting and beautiful face—so filled with warmth and humbleness. Somehow as I looked at him, I felt I was seeing Hawaiʻi as I'd never seen it before . . . ."

PHOTO BY JERRY Y. CHONG

News photographer Jerry Y. Chong's birthday is August 24—the same as Duke's. For many years, his assignment was to go to Duke's party and take his photo. There were 6,000 people at his 77th birthday party. Don Ho said it was "the biggest party he had ever been to."

In a 1995 interview, Waikīkī resident 92-year-old Joseph L. Brennan offered insight into the enigmatic world champion's reluctance to seek publicity.

Duke was a longtime member of the Los Angeles Athletic Club. Brennan, aspiring to be a boxer, joined the Club in the 1920s. He remembers looking down past his punching bag and seeing Duke at the pool. He was working on his starting dives with his trainer.

"I was very excited and said to my trainer, 'Mr. Blake, that has to be Duke!'

"Mr. B. said, 'Don't you go near him. Don't you go bothering him. He's the world's champ.'

"Well, of course I wasn't going to take any notice of Mr. B. I saw how to make a few bucks by writing a magazine story. I went looking for Duke later and asked him if I could interview him.'

"Duke said 'NO' very emphatically.

"I wouldn't take that for an answer. Whoever heard of a world champ turning down publicity? I asked him, 'Why not?'

"He said, 'There is an old Hawaiian superstition that if you write about someone when they're living, then they go *make*.'

"'What's that?' I asked.

"'That's M-A-K-E. Means die.' That was the end of my first 'interview' with Duke."

Duke not only declined offers for biographies, but also offers for statues, for the same reason.

A *Houston Chronicle* reporter interviewing Duke in April 1966 described him as "the only living legend in the world."

Writer Joseph Brennan sits with some of his books at his Waikīkī home. Behind him is a copy of Margaret D. Keane's portrait of Duke. It was painted in late 1967 and was the last for which he sat.

PHOTO BY SANDRA K. HALL

'Ohana

World-famous for his Olympic swimming performances, a hero to the Australians and others he taught to surf, a friend of royalty, Presidents, and Hollywood stars, Duke was most at home in Hawai'i, among his family and friends and close to the ocean he loved, where he paddled, sailed, and fished, as well as swam and surfed. Duke spoke Hawaiian; he loved the hula; and he embodied Hawai'i's spirit of Aloha.

Duke and Nadine on their arrival in Honolulu in January 1957 after the Melbourne Olympics. Duke saw Australia emerge triumphant in the medal count. Now that Hawai'i no longer dominated Olympic swimming, the U. S. won only one gold medal.

Duke Paoa Kahanamoku was born at Haleakalā, in downtown Honolulu, on August 24, 1890. At the time of Duke's birth, the City Directory listed his young father's occupation as clerk with the United Carriage Company. His next occupation, also unskilled, was as a delivery clerk in 1896 for a household goods dealer.

For the next 20 years, Duke, Sr., worked for the Honolulu Police Department. He started as a booking clerk and was steadily promoted through the ranks to Captain in 1911. In 1915 he resigned. He died within 2 years at 48, leaving a widow with 9 children, ages 6 to 27, of whom Duke was the oldest. In addition to the 6 boys there were 3 girls—Bernice, Kapiʻolani, and Maria.

The Kahanamoku brothers line up for their photo in 1928. Left to right, William, Samuel, Louis, David, Sargent, and Duke. They referred to each other as Brother, for example, Brother Sam. Duke was usually referred to as Brother Paoa.

The brothers 26 years later. By then, their get-togethers were less frequent. Some lived on neighbor islands. Sargent, the youngest and last surviving brother, died in 1993, at age 83. Left to right, Duke, David, Louis, Samuel, Sargent, and William.

COURTESY BURL BURLINGAME AIRCHIVE

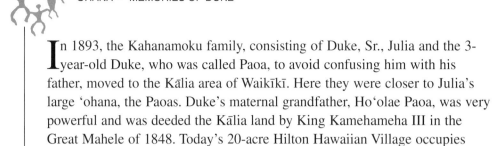

In 1893, the Kahanamoku family, consisting of Duke, Sr., Julia and the 3-year-old Duke, who was called Paoa, to avoid confusing him with his father, moved to the Kālia area of Waikīkī. Here they were closer to Julia's large 'ohana, the Paoas. Duke's maternal grandfather, Ho'olae Paoa, was very powerful and was deeded the Kālia land by King Kamehameha III in the Great Mahele of 1848. Today's 20-acre Hilton Hawaiian Village occupies much of this land. The Paoa land stretched from today's Ilikai Hotel Nikko Waikīkī on Ala Moana Boulevard to Kālia Road.

At one time there were more than 100 Paoas living in Kālia. Duke counted 31 Paoa cousins of his generation. None of the homes were fancy, like the homes in downtown Honolulu. A stream cut across the land; where it emptied into the ocean were extensive mudflats. Throughout Waikīkī and Kālia were ricefields, duck ponds, coconut groves, fish ponds and lagoons. Brother Louis once commented that they had gardens and grew enough taro and sweet potatoes to meet their needs. Both Hawaiian and English were spoken; many of the elders preferred Hawaiian.

Duke could always find someone to go fishing with, or swimming, or paddling. He was expected to catch fish, squid, shrimp and lobster for the ever-expanding family. He and his brothers were experts at traditional throw net fishing.

COURTESY *HONOLULU STAR-BULLETIN*

The Hilton Hawaiian Village was built on land that once belonged to Duke's mother's family. The City Planning Commission voted to name the man-made beach after Duke in 1956. Paoa Lane, a lane off Kālia Road, behind the Hilton, is another reminder of the days when the 'ohana lived there. A Hilton suite in the Rainbow Tower is named for Duke. Elvis always stayed there.

PHOTO BY WILLIAMS, COURTESY BISHOP MUSEUM

In this photograph, taken at the home of Maluhi Reis, Mauna'ihi Place, Honolulu, Duke's mother, Julia (third row, second from left), is in her early 60s. She is shown with members of the Daughters and Sons of Hawaiian Warriors, whose membership was open to descendants of Hawaiian ali'i. Julia was involved with many community organizations, and was a volunteer for the Red Cross and Lē'ahi and Kapi'olani hospitals.

COURTESY KAMEHAMEHA SCHOOLS/BISHOP ESTATE

Member of the Kamehameha School's 1908 championship soccer team, Duke is second from right, back row. The team won 5 of its 6 games. Duke also played football and basketball and competed in track. In 1961 he received the Ke Ali'i Pauahi Award—Kamehameha School's highest honor.

"The Kahanamoku family grew up in an area near Hilton Hawaiian Village, near my grandmother's house, which was next to the Royal Hawaiian," says Kimo Wilder McVay, Duke's personal manager for the last seven years of his life.

"He taught my mother [Kīna'u Wilder] to swim in Waikīkī in 1906, when she was only six or seven years old. My mother said he was the most magnificent human male that God ever put on the Earth. When he was young he was built like a bronzed Adonis. She was just a little girl and he was in his teens, and my mother was enchanted."

◆

"The funniest thing he told me happened when he was [working at the docks as a stevedore and] a diver," says former Waikīkī beachboy George Downing. "They were setting pilings down at Honolulu Harbor and they had these cranes that were bringing pilings. Duke was hired as one of the hard-hat divers. They would send a piling down and Duke would set it upright, and they would start hammering it in.

"So once they set the first one they would keep a line around it to hold it. He was down there waiting, and nothing came down. So he took the line he had to secure the piling, and he secured himself, and he fell asleep, sound asleep under water. So these guys had a message line to his helmet that they could jerk on, and they were jerking away and the line was tied up. So they sent a skindiver down to take a look, and Duke was sound asleep."

George "Keoki" Downing, winner of countless surfing championships in both hemispheres, is one of the pioneering crusaders for saving the oceans.

Duke was as handsome at 40 as he was at 16.

PHOTO BY TAI SING LOO, COURTESY BISHOP MUSEUM

"The King of the Water was hailed a national hero when he showed he could handle unaided a big outrigger [canoe], similar to the one which sturdy Kamehameha, ancient king of the islands, used to man alone. "Ordinarily four natives are barely able to launch such a boat."

(Unattributed clip from 1912, in the Hawai'i State Archives)

◆

To many people, Duke's greatest talent was swimming; to others, it was surfing. But Waikīkī beachboy and surfing great Rabbit Kekai saw Duke differently. "Paddling was Duke's forte; he was a better paddler and steersman than surfer."

Rabbit also was a natural at steering canoes, and attracted Duke's attention when he won his first race at age 11 as a junior steersman. "Duke took a liking to me; he taught me a lot of things, saying everything in Hawaiian."

At 12, Rabbit earned the honor of becoming a top steersman for Hui Nalu. And then he got a chance to show his teacher what an apt pupil he was. "I won the junior race; we were beating the Outrigger Canoe Club in everything. But senior steersman Blue Makua . . . got tossed in jail, so for the senior race I had to go up against Duke. Back then he won every race; you couldn't beat Duke.

"Duke was ahead of us in a three-mile race, and we were a canoe length behind. He caught a wave, I caught a wave, he was on it, then I was on it. We were coming in to the last turn, and we got closer to him. I was on the outside and Duke was smart to get on the inside; here is the finish line so if you get the inside you win it. But we're both on the same wave so I swung way outside of him. I saw Duke go close to the buoy and I knew he was going to swing wide. So I told the guys to slow down and they thought I was crazy. Sure enough I saw Duke swing wide and I went straight for the buoy and we had the inside and we ran in and beat him. Duke taught me that.

"When I went up to get the trophy, the whole Kahanamoku family shook my hand. And Duke said, 'You remembered.'

"So my coach asked me, 'Where did you learn that?' and I said, 'Duke taught me that a long time ago.' And he said, 'Whatever Duke tells you, you remember.'"

COURTESY BISHOP MUSEUM

Duke was a fine paddler and paddling coach. In the 1940s, he put together a team of six teenagers who had been hanging around the Outrigger Canoe Club. In one month they defeated six other teams for the Walter MacFarlane trophy. For the next five years, this core group, plus others, with Duke at the helm, won every trophy.

In February 1917, Duke showed his athletic versatility at the 21st annual Labor Day Regatta when he won the senior single sliding-seat scull race with ease, 5 boat lengths ahead of his nearest rival.

The Regatta's most exciting event was the Senior Six race between 3 clubs: the Healani Blues, winner for the past 7 years, the Myrtle Reds and Hilo. Duke was steersman for the Myrtles. The winner of the 2-mile race would be state champion.

A lot of money changed hands the week before the regatta. Most saw the contest as Healani versus Hilo. Some wagers were as much as $1000 on Healani. Later in the week, when the Myrtles said they favored Healani over Hilo, betting became feverish. What they had not counted on was the sleek new barge that the Myrtles would be rowing for the first time.

The Myrtles' new barge was as yet unnamed. Several wags suggested Chilly Maru and Sub Rosa, after club official Bill Rosa. Another suggestion was K. Duke, "Inasmuch as Duke is about the fastest thing in the water." Attorney Charley Davis, who donated the most money, was asked to select a name, and he chose Duke P. Kahanamoku.

Duke was honored. When the race got underway in the Harbor the barges were out of sight. Myrtles rowed in the center lane and "Duke's shining bronze body stood out from the rest as the sun glistened on it. He wore a sailor hat—by now one of his trademarks."

In a very close race, Duke pushed his crew to finish with several hard strokes just ahead of Hilo. It reminded spectators of the way Duke finished his swimming races—he always paced himself and kept enough energy in reserve to win.

(*Honolulu Star-Bulletin*, September 11, 1917)

When he won the senior single sliding-seat scull race at the 1917 Honolulu Regatta, Duke was heralded as the best rower in the islands. The sculls, popularized by King Kalākaua, were modeled on English rowing skiffs.

Duke returned from California to live in Honolulu during the Depression. He was pleased when a position was created for him by newly elected Mayor George F. Wright. The job, Superintendent of City Hall, was at least a job, although it really just meant being a glorified janitor. It did not last long. Duke was unceremoniously "kicked out," said an indignant editorial in the February 18, 1933, *Honolulu Star-Bulletin*, by the newly seated Democratic majority of the board of supervisors.

Senator David K. Trask, angry at his own party, introduced a bill to give him a pension for life of $350 per month, double his terminating salary—but he could not muster the votes.

Jobs were scarce in 1929-30, when Duke returned to Honolulu. He lived at home with his mother until he was offered a city job. One job was to cut the grass. He was deemed the "grass-mowing champion" of the city, although he was frequently interrupted by friends wanting to talk story as he worked. The reporter joked that he did the mowing at lunchtime so that people could see that he was working hard and earning his salary.

Duke was crew for Harold G. Dillingham in the 1934 Trans-Pacific Yacht Race, which they won on handicap. As the yacht approached Moloka'i, a navy plane dropped leis and poi. Duke had been without poi for 13 days—and without a razor! Duke often said that he was one of the first people to have ever crossed the ocean from Hawai'i to California the four possible ways: by sail, by steamer, by oil-fired engine, and by airplane.

July 1934 was a great month for Duke—he was a crew member of the winner of the Trans-Pacific Yacht Race, and then, costumed as Kamehameha the Great, welcomed U.S. President Franklin D. Roosevelt to Honolulu.

Duke was one of a crew of 8 on Harold G. Dillingham's 61-foot yacht, *Manu'iwa*. The boat took second-place line honors in the grueling 2,200-mile race from San Pedro, California, to Honolulu, but first place by handicap.

The details of the race were imprinted on his mind. Fifteen years later, in a July 19, 1949, radio interview with Lowell Thomas, he explained how the elapsed time of 13 days, 12 hours, 30 minutes, 51 seconds corrected to 12 days, 9 hours, 29 minutes, and 56 seconds to give the *Manu'iwa* first-place honors.

Duke was a sheriff who never fired his gun. He ran for the office of Sheriff of the City and County of Honolulu in 1934, defeating his experienced Republican opponent by a sizable majority. His 13 consecutive terms in office—until the office was abolished—is yet another record Duke racked up. After his fourth election, he switched political parties and was still elected.

Nadine remembers, "He really liked his job. He was in charge of weights and measures, the coroner's office, transportation of indigent dead, process serving, transporting prisoners to court and hospital, and the old Iwilei jail. He did a very good job.

"He had to run for office every two years, although he really never was a politician. He only once had an opponent. It got to the point where people would think, "What's the point in running against him. He's so adored, he's unbeatable." In 1956 he was absent, in Australia, during the election. He did

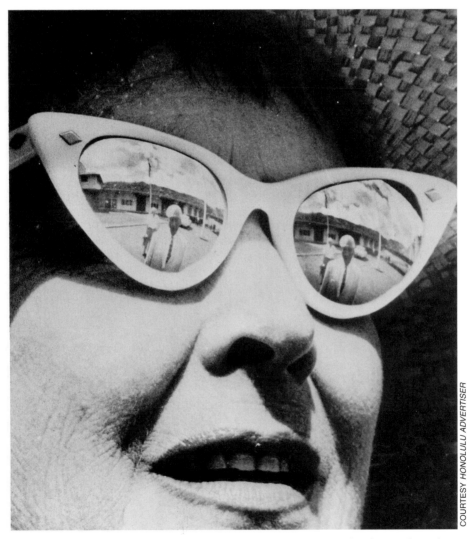

Duke's top priority as Sheriff was construction of a new municipal jail to replace the inadequate one in Iwilei, built in 1857. A new jail became Duke's standing request to the legislature. In 1962, the new Halawa facility was opened, after Duke's position had been eliminated with the new state charter. The jail is reflected in Nadine's sunglasses.

no campaigning, but he was elected just the same!

"When he gave a speech—usually about the need for a new jail, inmate rehabilitation, things like that—he'd always start his speech in Hawaiian, then he'd switch to English. The old Hawaiians loved to hear him speak Hawaiian."

"He was very, very pleased when the new prison was built. He had traveled extensively around the mainland visiting jails, getting ideas."

(*Honolulu*, December 1988, and interview by author in 1995)

◆

Sandwiched between his Hollywood years and his nearly three decades as sheriff was a two-year stint as a gas station operator. He leased two Union stations—one on Nu'uanu at Pauoa, the other on Kalākaua at Seaside, opposite the Royal Hawaiian Hotel. His brother Samuel worked for him as an attendant.

Business was very competitive; to give himself an edge, he promoted his famous name on—what else?—a surfboard. He landscaped the tiny garden with bright hibiscus and other tropical plants. Tourists and *kama'āina* loved to drive in for gas, say "Aloha," and have him pose for a photograph.

Duke rented an apartment nearby on Seaside Avenue so that when work was *pau*, he could grab a bite to eat, change into his swimsuit, and be out surfing within minutes.

PHOTO BY HOWARD HILL, COURTESY BISHOP MUSEUM

For a couple of years, Duke leased two gasoline stations. He put up with a lot of teasing, including a song written about him, called "Duke, Former Olympic Champion, Now Pumping Gas."

107

HE—one of the world's most famous, handsome, eligible bachelors, never married, age 50.

SHE—Nadine Alexander (pronounced NAH-deen, not NAYdeen), professional dancer and instructor, former owner of London and New York dance studios, extroverted, beautiful, sophisticated, divorced, age 35.

DESTINY—She arrived in Honolulu, realized that Duke was the man whose photo she had seen in a magazine and fallen in love with during her school days.

Their versions of how and when they met are a little inconsistent, like those of many long-married couples.

Their stories:

HIS: "One day in 1940 I was on the beach at Waikīkī and I saw her on the lanai of the Royal Hawaiian Hotel. It sort of struck me. Like, she's my girl. So I asked my brother Sam, who was with her, to introduce me, and that was the beginning of our romance.

"Later she taught me to dance. She said she had loved me since she first saw me in that movie magazine.

HERS: "Because my parents were theatrical—my father was a headliner in vaudeville in the United States and Europe, and my mother was an opera singer in Australia—I read movie magazines. I was just a teenager in high school when a photograph of a newly discovered star caught my eye. I read the article about how Douglas Fairbanks, Sr., and his wife, Mary Pickford, were helping launch the career of this very handsome new Polynesian actor."

His picture was imprinted on her memory for more than twenty years. She forgot his strange Hawaiian name, but did remember "Duke."

(Bob Krauss, *Honolulu Advertiser*, August 3, 1965, and 1993 interview by author)

Left to right, Douglas Fairbanks, unidentified man, Mary Pickford, and Duke, at the Royal Hawaiian Hotel in 1929. Duke had returned to Honolulu to spend Christmas with his mother and look for a job. Although Doug and Mary stayed only overnight, Duke and Doug fitted in a lively game of golf at Waiʻalae Country Club.

Years later, after returning to the United States from Europe, Nadine was offered a position in Honolulu teaching ballroom dancing. The studio was at the Royal Hawaiian Hotel; she lived next door at the Moana.

Using the stage name Norma Allen, the glamorous Nadine arrived in Honolulu December 1938 on the SS *Lurline*. She waited by the purser's door where Harold "Andy" Anderson, co-owner of the Boleyn-Anderson Dance Studio, met her. She noticed an attractive young couple standing on the pier. Nadine asked Andy, "Who is that dark man with the blonde woman?" He replied, "Why, that's Sargent Kahanamoku and Jane Topping."

When she was told, the name "Kahanamoku" clicked, but she thought the first name should be "Duke." Andy explained that Sarge and Duke were brothers, adding, "Duke swims every day after work at the Outrigger Canoe Club at 4:00 p.m."

She remembers, "Of course back then, the Outrigger was right next to the Royal Hawaiian Hotel where the dance studio was, so I knew it was just a matter of time . . . ."

Nadine settled in and began teaching, specializing in Latin dancing. Her pupils were from Hawai'i's "Big Five" trade and agriculture companies, and the Royal Hawaiian's clientele. "It was not too long before I met Sam, Louis, and then Bill . . . all the brothers except David and Duke. Finally I said, 'Sam, I want to meet your brother Duke.'"

She remembers, "My heart went pitty-pat when I saw him. He had a magnificent physique, and a mane of steel-gray hair."

"For me, it had been love at first sight. He seemed more cautious, a confirmed bachelor. It took a few days for Duke to get up the courage to invite me to dinner. He was afraid I'd reject him, he told me later."

(Bob Krauss, *Honolulu Advertiser*, August 3, 1965, and 1993 interview by author)

The newspapers reported the arrival on the Lurline *of the accomplished dancer "Norma Allen." Later, she wished she had chosen a different name. "Why didn't I choose Arlen, or something like that?" she asked the author in 1995. "For a while I had been engaged to Harold Arlen, the lyricist, and that would have been a fun name to hide behind. He would not have minded."*

Nadine remembers their courtship:

"On our first date, he came by and picked me up in his car. We had dinner at Wo Fat's Restaurant, in Chinatown. Nothing fancy, but very exotic! A real thrill being together at long last!

"We dated for a few months. He decided I was 'The One for him' when he thought I was going to marry someone else."

Was she going to marry somebody else?

"One of my dancing pupils was much younger than Duke and very wealthy, and he begged me to marry him and move to the mainland.

"I was confused. I was so in love with the Islands and with Duke. But he hadn't proposed. I went to the Big Island to spend Christmas [1939] with friends. While I was there, I called Duke to wish him a Merry Christmas. I told him I had gotten this marriage proposal."

He proposed, by telephone:

"All Duke said was 'Baby, come home.' Just like that. I knew what he meant. So I did. I came home to O'ahu and my one and only Duke."

They married:

"Eight months later we married, on August 2, 1940. In those days, that was a whirlwind romance. We decided to keep the wedding a secret, because otherwise all Hawai'i *nei* would expect to be invited. We slipped away from Honolulu by inter-island plane to Kailua-Kona, on the Big Island. His sister Bernice, who was very, very close to Duke and whom he loved dearly, was so excited that she leaked the news to the radio station that Duke was getting married. As we drove to Mokua'ikaua Church we turned on the radio. We were surprised to hear an announcement that we were already wed! That's how she kept the secret!

"We were married by the Reverend Stephen Desha. We didn't dress up—I had been married before when I was very young. Actually, I had eloped with a Harvard dental school graduate, who was also a musician. Duke had never been married before, so I wanted to do it his way, and of course, he didn't want a big fuss.

"Duke gave me forty pīkake leis! He told me it was the most a bride had ever worn. I thought that was very romantic and very Hawaiian.

"Our attendants were Francis I'i Brown, Duke's best friend, and Francis's lady companion, Winona Love, a fine hula dancer and movie star, and Bernice Kahanamoku.

"Nobody remembered to bring a camera—can you imagine? If it hadn't been for the Kona Inn bartender, we wouldn't have had any photographs! Afterwards, we had a little party with a few close friends."

(Bob Krauss, *Honolulu Advertiser*, August 3, 1965, and 1995 interview with author)

Mr. and Mrs. Duke Kahanamoku after their marriage, August 2, 1940. Nadine said that Duke had just kissed her, and that is why her hat is at a jaunty angle.

Nadine remembers the honeymoon:

"We honeymooned at Brown's isolated estate, Keawaiki, on the Kohala Coast. The setting was idyllic. Right on the ocean, ancient fish ponds, lava fields and white beaches. The only way to get there was by ship or by horseback—there were no roads.

"The accommodations made us laugh. There was a generator to make electricity. No telephones. We stayed in a sort of shed where Francis kept his fishing nets. It had a chest of drawers and two cots. Duke was over six feet tall and his feet hung over the end of the bed. We put the two cots together so we could be together. That didn't work, and we'd fall down in the middle. The tin roof reverberated to the slightest scratch of a palm frond, so we didn't sleep very well.

"Every morning before the sun came up, Francis would throw stones on the roof to wake Duke. He'd jump up, have a cup of coffee, and the two of

Mele Kalikimaka
Makahiki Hou

NADINE and DUKE KAHANAMOKU

The newlyweds' Christmas card, the first year they were married.

them would go out fishing. All day, every day. You'd think they were the honeymooners!

"I was left with Winona all day. With chickens scurrying around everywhere, that meant fresh eggs for breakfast—but someone had to climb a coconut palm to get them. The chickens roosted way up in the trees, to stop the mongooses from stealing the eggs!

"Winona I think resented me because I was a *haole* girl. She was polite and nice, but I did not feel accepted.

"Although we were on our honeymoon, Duke worked—he laid out and paved some paths for Francis. Duke was like that. He liked to do things for his friends. They always called the paths 'Duke's Highway.'"

◆

And they lived happily ever after:

Nadine remembers:
"When Duke was single, he had rented a house at the foot of Diamond Head. Later, we bought a house on Royal Circle. Fortunately, Doris Duke helped us with an interest-free loan, as Duke had no money. Duke lived here the rest of his life. We paid back the loan by monthly payments as rent.

"After we were married, many *tūtūs* came up to me, pointed their fingers and said, 'You look after our boy,' and 'You be good to our Duke!' They scared me half to death!

"I told Duke before we got married that I could not have children; he couldn't care less. He was not about to give me up."

COURTESY BURL BURLINGAME AIRCHIVE

Both Nadine and Duke loved dogs. Here Duke greets a new puppy that was shipped to him as a gift by Los Angeles friends, before he was married. He met the dog at the wharf with a puppy-sized lei and a jingle toy, before it was sent off to quarantine.

Nadine remembers:

"He was a devoted husband. He wrote me many endearing letters and telegrams. We were married for 27 years. We called each other 'Baby.' The last years were sometimes hard, and I worried a lot, with all his health troubles.

"The only time that Duke got really, really, angry with me was when I was in the movie *South Pacific*. I had a bit part as a nun—so bitty, if you blink you'll miss me. We were on location on Kaua'i. I was between shoots. I went swimming alone, got beyond my depth, and nearly drowned. When I told Duke about it, he scolded me, 'Never, never, never swim alone. The currents are too tricky.'

"He was always so sweet. I used to be a chainsmoker—three packs a day. I gave it up over Lent. It was really hard. I asked him if he was glad I had stopped.

"He said 'Baby, I always disliked your smoking. It made everything—my clothes, the house—smell of smoke. I'm glad you quit.' I asked him why he'd never said anything. He shrugged and said, 'Because it gave you so much pleasure.'"

Nadine had appeared in several movies in France. Here she plays a nun in South Pacific.

Nadine was the right kind of woman for Duke. Highly intelligent, savvy in business, assertive, with a quick sense of humor, and at ease socially with people from all walks of life.

Socializing and entertaining came easily to her. She loved singing, literature, music, ballet, and the theater. Like Duke, she loved to travel. She had traveled alone to places like Casablanca and Marrakech, Morocco, France and Italy. She had been in every state of the union with her traveling show-business family before she was 6 years old. Her first visit to Hawai'i was when she was 5, on her way to visit her Australian grandmother. She distinctly remembered the boys diving for money in Honolulu Harbor and dining at the Moana Hotel.

Nadine remembers married life:

Did he help much around the house? He described his role: Nadine fixed dinner and shooed him out of the kitchen. Then Duke shooed her out of the kitchen while he did the dishes.

"He was a handyman and gardener. He had a couple of funny stories that made the papers. One headline was 'Sheriff Loses Bout With Cactus.' He was trimming a tree, lost his balance, and fell backward. He tried to break his fall by grabbing a cactus. He was checked at the hospital emergency room, was okay, except that his hands stung. It took weeks for all the spikes to work their way out!"

Another time, when Nadine was on the mainland, he locked himself out of the house. When he got home that night, he put the ladder against the side, climbed up and entered through a second-story window. "He always thought that this was very funny, that the sheriff had to break into his house, and wondered what would have happened if someone had seen him and called the police."

Duke forgot their silver wedding anniversary. He told the *Honolulu Advertiser's* Bob Krauss, "I don't know what to get her. What if I get her something she doesn't like?"

(Bob Krauss, *Honolulu Advertiser,* August 3, 1965)

COURTESY PACIFIC AEROSPACE MUSEUM, PAN AM COLLECTION

With her fine features, her baby-fine brown hair, eyes as blue and captivating as the Waikīkī surf, and an enchanting smile, she was a "head turner." The 35-year-old Nadine and 50-year-old Duke were one of the world's most striking couples.

Duke's Favorite Food:

As a young man—poi.
As a married man, after dining in the world's finest restaurants—poi.
Corned beef and raw onions, with poi or rice.
Cold canned salmon with poi, and an onion, quartered.
More poi.

Duke loved poi so much that his friends often kidded him about it. In the early years, the family grew enough taro for their needs on their Kālia land.

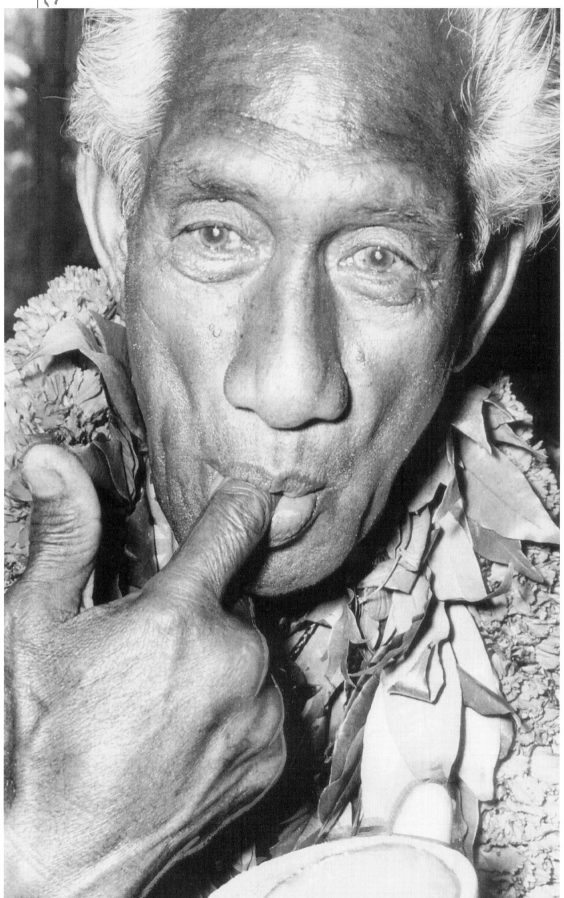

Nadine really appreciated that Duke was a natural dancer. She recalled how other people would stop dancing to watch them. He learned all the dances—the foxtrot, rhumba, tango, shag, Lambeth Walk. He was also a very fine hula dancer. On special occasions he would dance the "Holoholo Ka'a" (Going my way, automobile).

COURTESY LIBRARY OF CONGRESS, PRINTS AND PHOTOGRAPHS DIVISION, NYWT&S COLLECTION

This picture of Duke "The hot-shot hula dancer" went out over the wire service in September 1936. His partner is the famous dancer Aggie Auld. Duke has his jacket tied around his waist to represent a hula skirt.

COURTESY HONOLULU STAR-BULLETIN

Some of the crowd of about 200 oldtimers gathered near the hau trees at Waikīkī to celebrate "Dad" Center's birthday. The lei-bedecked 67-year-old Center dances an impromptu hula with the 63-year-old Duke. As young men, Center and Duke competed in rowing, swimming and paddleboard races. Center was a Swimming Hall of Fame inductee.

COURTESY *HONOLULU ADVERTISER*

*On his 76th birthday , Duke danced the hula. His cake featured a picture of his dancing with the Queen Mother. He was presented with many gifts, including a Rolls Royce, and a plaque from the Hawai'i Visitors' Bureau (HVB). "We give you this plaque," said Bob Allen, because you made the HVB possible." (*Honolulu Advertiser, *August 25, 1966)*

119

With age, Duke graduated from his longboard to a 10-foot fiberglass board with skegs that was lighter for carrying and more maneuverable in the waves.

Then he traded his board for boats. First sailboats, finally power boats. He owned a variety in the last two decades of his life, a sleek yacht, a catamaran, and two cruisers. The cruisers were both called *Nadu K*, from a combination of the first letters of his and Nadine's names.

Because the catamaran was a variation of the Hawaiian double-hulled outrigger canoe that Duke had grown up with, he was very adept at sailing it. He wrote to close friend Arthur Godfrey:

"Boy, you have not experienced anything more thrilling. Imagine sailing along on a 20-foot boat at better than 20 knots without motor-power of any kind but the wind. It's ice sailing on the ocean. The craze, I am sure, will eventually hit the mainland. I'm hoping that I can ship my 'cat' up to San Pedro and be playing around there at the start of the Trans-Pacific Yacht Race on July 4th, 1955. Boy, it will open their eyes to see the thing sail rings around most anything. I know you'll get a tremendous kick out of it."

COURTESY *HONOLULU STAR-BULLETIN*

Duke enjoyed everything about boats—puttering around them, fishing from them, racing, and leisure sailing. His activities were curtailed during World War II, but as soon as the war was over and curfews and restrictions lifted, he helped found the Waikiki Yacht Club.

"I remember I went sailing with him one time on this 26-foot catamaran that Woody Brown had made," says surfing great and former Waikīkī beachboy George Downing. "We were out sailing and the wind went down, the sail started to luff. I said to him, 'What do you want to do, pull in the sheet?' And he said, 'No, the *makani* come.' So he looked up and kind of whistled. And sure enough, before you know it, the wind started blowing again, and we got past that little dead spot off Diamond Head. He just loved being in the water, out in the boat."

Duke with his 596-lb. catch at the Hawaiian International Billfish Tournament. In honor of Duke, a huge wooden perpetual trophy carved in the likeness of a billfish is awarded to the person who boats the biggest fish at the tournament, held in Kona each summer.

Duke loved fishing. Some of his happiest days in his later years were spent fishing on his boat. Kenneth Francis Brown, nephew of Francis Iʻi Brown, Duke's best friend, remembers Duke fishing in the Hawaiian International Billfish Competition.

Clubs from around the world compete against each other. The total weight of blue marlin caught by the four-person team determines the winner. Duke had fished in the tournament for many years with Brown and the Kawaiahae Fishing Club. Duke was always running the vessel instead of fishing.

"Our crew was fighting for the lead against two others. The big blue Duke hooked would have guaranteed the lead. I told him to tighten the drag because the fish was sounding. He tightened it all the way, gave a mighty heave, and broke the rod in three places. That disqualified him, but it shows you how incredibly strong he was at 71!

"It didn't even bother him that he broke the rod," said Brown. "We boated the fish, instead of cutting the line, and took it in for weighing. It weighed 596 pounds—an impressive catch. Duke wore the rod around his neck like a lei."

(*Honolulu Advertiser,* August 22, 1979)

Up to the end of his life, he said, "I like the feel of the fresh air and the salt water. I believe in keeping active."

But surgery to remove a cerebral clot put an end to solo sailing on his catamaran, as he was not as nimble as before. His doctor suspected that the clot had been caused by an encounter with the boom.

He called the new hole in his skull a *puka.* Joe Brennan said, "A plastic plate was put in. I'd visit him in hospital, and he'd say, "'Hey, Cho, feel this.'"

COURTESY HONOLULU ADVERTISER

This photograph was taken after Duke had undergone surgery to remove a cerebral clot. It had spread over 10 percent of his brain and caused dizziness and violent headaches. The delicate experimental angiography surgery was a total success, although he was in critical condition for a week. Keeping him motivated during his long recuperation was his desire to walk without a cane and to be fit enough to swim.

COURTESY *HONOLULU ADVERTISER*

Duke had a much-admired, full head of hair all his life, even after brain surgery. It was black, then steel gray, then finally a "snow-white mane." He said that all the Kahanamokus had good hair because their mother used to put herbs in a cloth and squeeze them on their hair.

Duke worked quietly "behind the scenes" to promote Native Hawaiian issues. Seven years before Hawai'i achieved statehood, he wrote to Mino'aka (his close friend Arthur Godfrey):

"We are crossing our fingers in high hopes that one of our boys, the Hon. Samuel Wilder King, be appointed Governor of Hawai'i. Should this materialize it would signal for every Hawaiian to rejoice, because it would be the very first time since 1898 [55 years ago], when a Native Hawaiian is selected for the high post.

"To us, we feel that this is 'full recognition' of our citizenship in this Great Country. Up to this point it has been a case of 'you Hawaiians can go so far and then stop' while everybody else was being given consideration."

◆

Governor John A. Burns (Governor from 1962-1974) proclaimed Duke's 73rd birthday, August 24, 1963, "Duke Kahanamoku Day." The formal dinner at the Royal Hawaiian Hotel was attended by 200 guests, including the mayor, Republican Neal Blaisdell.

Mrs. Kīna'u Wilder gave Duke a rare feather cloak that had been in her family for 30 years. Monseigneur Charles Kekumano announced the formation of the Outrigger Duke Kahanamoku Foundation to provide scholarships for student athletes, which pleased Duke enormously.

Duke dressed as an ali'i for the 1917 Washington Day Festival. He rode a surfboard on a simulated wave on a float in the parade. Duke lived through profound changes in the Hawaiian nation—through royalty, republic, territory, and state.

COURTESY HONOLULU STAR-BULLETIN

The organizers of Hilo's first Merrie Monarch Festival were thrilled and relieved that Duke brought clear skies and sunshine with him. Duke alighted from the official limousine at the reviewing stand with his usual dignity and poise, in his stocking feet, with his shoes in his hand. He put his shoes on, walked to his seat, sat down, and proceeded to take his shoes off again.

COURTESY HONOLULU STAR-BULLETIN

Two dignitaries get together to salute Duke on his 73rd birthday. Left to right, Governor John A. Burns, Duke, and Mayor of the City and County of Honolulu, Neal S. Blaisdell.

125

"He was totally at peace," says George Downing. "He had gone through life and was now just reflecting back, through his endeavors as an athlete, his business experiences, his being a movie actor, his experiences as a socialite, you name it.

So when he came home, he was like a little kid. I saw the little boy in him; he never lost this feeling of being part of this Hawaiian way. He was proud of it, he was good at it. He seemed to be enthusiastic about it. Even as he got older, he was stoked.

When he went surfing he was stoked. When he went in a canoe or sailing, he was stoked. That was his gift.

The boy remained in him always. That's the thing I saw."

Taken on his 64th birthday, this is possibly the last photograph of Duke surfing. Renowned surfing photographer Clarence "Mac" Maki, who snapped the photo in 1954, recalls how Duke said, "Mac, got any film yet? It's my birthday today." Luckily, Maki had two frames left.

126

COURTESY EASTER SEAL SOCIETY OF HAWAII

To the end, Duke gave of his time to children. He had special aloha for children who faced challenges; he was involved with the cystic fibrosis, tuberculosis, and Easter Seal campaigns. Here he poses with four-year-old Alan Nagao, who was the local and national Easter Seal child for 1966. Alan spontaneously gave Duke this kiss and hug. Some of the last photographs Duke posed for were with Easter Seal children. His widow and Charlie Wedemeyer are the Honorary Co-Chairs for the 1996 Fiftieth Capital Campaign.

"Aloha, aloha," smiled Duke, shuffling in, "Mele Kalīkimaka!" It was a month before Duke died. Eddie Sherman's four-year-old part-Hawaiian adopted son, Shawn, was playing with his new train set when Duke and Nadine arrived.

Sherman remembered, "For the next two hours, Duke sat fascinated, absorbed with my son in the mechanical wonder of the train . . . . They played, laughed and communicated . . . . Watching the two, the beautiful simplicity of the man shone—as always—like a beacon . . . . In this day of pseudo ultra-sophistication, this unaffected quality was a joy to behold . . . .

"It was honest. It was true. It was majestic. It was Ali'i."

(*Honolulu Advertiser*, January 24, 1968)

◆

"I used to try to get him to smile, so one day, I thought, 'Gee, what is the best question you could ask somebody like Duke?'" says former Waikīkī beachboy and surfing great George Downing. "There were two things I always felt were right to ask somebody of his stature. So at the right time, I asked him, 'Duke, if I were to say to you I could give you 100 more years of life, on one condition, that you would have to forget everything that you have experienced in your life, what would you say to me?' He said, 'Keoki, no way. The life that I've led, I would never give up that experience, the people I've met, the enjoyment I've had, for the future.' He was totally at peace."

Aloha

The world bid Duke "Aloha" on January 22, 1968. He was remembered in Congress and in national magazines and newspapers as a symbol of Hawai'i, as a man of many accomplishments who was at peace with himself. Today, statues honoring his excellence in swimming and surfing and his role as Ambassador of Aloha are shrines in California, Hawai'i, and elsewhere, and those who knew him still remember his sportsmanship, his honesty, and his kindness.

January 27, 1968, a solemn day at Waikīkī for Duke's funeral services

"DIED: Duke Kahanamoku, 77, Hawai'i's fabled swimmer, surfer and all-round citizen . . . his name might as well have been King: tall (6 ft. 2 in.), mahogany-skinned and magnificently muscled, a descendant of Polynesian royalty, Kahanamoku burst upon the athletic world in 1911 . . . , breaking the [100-yard freestyle] record . . . . His novel flutter kick outmoded the standard scissors kick overnight, and in the next 13 years he collected a slew of world records and three Olympic gold medals. That, plus his rescue of eight people from a capsized launch off the California coast in 1925, boosted a new career in Hollywood, but he returned home in 1929 and served 26 years as sheriff of Honolulu. Age never daunted him. To the last, he was a symbol of the islands, surfing, swimming, and appearing as the 50th state's official greeter."

(TIME Magazine, February 2, 1968)

Then-U.S. Congressman, later Senator Spark Matsunaga told a hushed Congress of Duke's death.

"The regal Duke has long been recognized as the world's number one Hawaiian.

"Just as Diamond Head symbolized the geography of Hawai'i, Duke symbolized the people of Hawai'i.

"More than any other individual, he represented what other people throughout the world picture the true Hawaiian to be— friendly, cheerful, athletic, tall, and handsome—someone you wanted to get to know better. He made you proud to even be just an acquaintance of his.

"The legendary Duke sold Hawai'i to the world and in so doing became a citizen of the world. Hawai'i, the United States and the whole human race have lost a true champion and a rare specimen of a man."

(*Congressional Record*, 90th Congress, 2nd Session, January 23, 1968)

A photo of Duke swimming in August 1967. It was transmitted with the Associated Press wire story announcing Duke's death.

COURTESY AP/WIDE WORLD PHOTOS

Duke's funeral took place five days after his death. There were Episcopal and Masonic rites, followed by beachboy services. Parts of the service were in English, parts in Hawaiian.

Duke and Arthur Godfrey had a pact—whoever died first, the other would deliver his friend's eulogy. Mino'aka (Duke's nickname for Godfrey), looking frail and overwhelmed, gave a brief eulogy for Duke:

"Duke was the soul of dignity . . . but he could be a mischievous, delightful boy at heart. And so he remained until his last moments . . . . He was unassuming, reticent, almost shy . . . . Flattery rolled off his back like spume from a wave . . . . He retreated from fawning phonies, politely but firmly . . . . It was the wonderful world of water that gave Duke his relaxed, enviable peace of mind . . . . That great physical strength alone would never have won those titles for him . . . . He had known defeat but he had persevered with great courage to overcome the weaknesses of human frailty. He was a great *ali'i*, who gave stature to Hawai'i *nei*."

(Arthur Godfrey, "Memories of a Great Man," *Beacon*, August 1968, pp. 21-23)

COURTESY HONOLULU ADVERTISER

Wreaths and leis are lovingly placed on the outrigger canoe that will transport Duke's urn for the traditional beachboy scattering of ashes ceremony. Arthur Godfrey is next to Nadine (in dark glasses).

The beach ceremony and scattering of the ashes were held in front of the Royal Hawaiian Hotel, near where he had surfed, trained, swum, frolicked, played his ukulele, first met his wife.

At the ceremony were people from every economic station in life, from millionaires to beachboys who probably did not have enough money for their next meal in their pocket; people of every ethnicity; sportsmen, couch potatoes, movie stars, *malihini, kama'āina.* There were bikinis, bare feet, Hawaiian ceremonial regalia, Masonic uniforms, suits, aloha shirts—every type of dress imaginable.

Waikīkī was so muted, quiet, and dark, it was almost unrecognizable. Hawaiians will tell you how it always rains at *ali'i's* funerals—at Princess Kai'ulani's, at Bernice Pauahi Bishop's. At Duke's, the storm clouds hovered, but held back their tears awhile.

Duke's canoe waited, with one of his surfboards decorated in flowers resting against it, while the Reverend Abraham Akaka, in a swimsuit, led a Hawaiian prayer. The beachboys serenaded with two of his favorite songs— the Hui Nalu song, and " 'Imi Au Iā 'Oe" (I am seeking you).

The canoe and lei-bedecked surfboard. The canoe took Duke's urn out past the surfing breaks he loved so well.

Thousands of mourners lined the beach at Waikīkī for Duke's funeral. A flotilla of canoes accompanied Duke's ashes. the heavens rained, the sea was agitated and uneasy. Duke's youngest brother, Sarge, said that manō, *Duke's* ʻaumakua, *circled them, a sign that Duke was being led home.*

Just as Duke had wanted it, 13 canoes paddled out in single file behind the canoe bearing his ashes. The clouds could not hold back the tears any longer. The rain began to fall as the canoes formed a circle. Rain and tears streamed down the mourners' faces as Duke returned to his ocean. The last private prayers were said, the flower leis were set afloat.

Then the paddlers felt Duke's presence. Many felt chickenskin creep up their arms. "I swear I could hear him humming Kui Lee's song 'One paddle, two paddle, three paddle . . . four to take me home . . . .' "

Someone shouted, "Let's go!"

The race was on! To the paddlers and the thousands on the beach, every wave, every stroke, the canoes flying through the water, personified who Duke was.

I overheard one tourist saying, "I have never seen anything so impressive."

(LeRae Britain, "We Miss You, Duke," *Beacon,* April 1972, pp. 13-14)

A tribute in the *Honolulu Advertiser,* January 23, 1968:

"When he turned 75 two years ago, we and others said the only question for history is how big Duke's legend will become.

"Some of the things bearing his name include a scholarship foundation, a beach, a swimming pool at the university, an annual regatta, a restaurant and a nightspot, a line of sportswear, a music and recording company, ukuleles, surfboards, a surfing club, and an international surfing championship.

"But far more important is perpetuating Duke's spirit—the friendly, modest young Hawaiian boy whose real accomplishments won the respect of the world, the older man who carried his legend with modest dignity. These are goals all might seek . . . .

"That Duke must always be a part of Hawai'i. It is a great sadness to lose him in body now. We must never lose him in spirit later."

———————————◆———————————

Huntington Beach, California, dedicated a bust and plaque to Duke in October 1969. This was 20 years before he was honored at Waikīkī.

The plaque reads:

"Duke Kahanamoku, Olympic swimmer, public servant, goodwill ambassador of the State of Hawai'i, and considered by many to be the father of modern surfing. In the early 1920s, the Duke surfed under this very pier. Some fifty years later he returned to this community to help promote the U.S. Surfboard Championships. For five consecutive years until his death, the championships were dedicated in honor of this man's contributions to the sport of surfing. The citizens of Huntington Beach have erected this monument as a tribute to the champion of champion surfers. The image he created, the principle of fair play and good sportsmanship he advocated should be preserved for all time. Although mortal man has lost this rare human being, he will always be remembered for his long aloha."

Duke's bust in the foyer of the International Surfing Hall of Fame in Huntington Beach, California. Duke was a frequent visitor to Huntington— as a young man he surfed there, and in his later years he officiated at surf meets.

PHOTO BY ELMAR BAXTER

135

***The New Yorker,* March 12, 1990, on the centennial of Duke's birth:**

"Duke was to swimming, what Babe Ruth and Joe DiMaggio COMBINED were to baseball."

Joe DiMaggio asks, "This is a bat?" DiMaggio was vacationing with Joe DiMaggio, Jr., in July 1953. He was the Outrigger Canoe Club's honorary marshal at the Walter MacFarlane Regatta. Elected to the Baseball Hall of Fame in 1955, the former Yankee great was Most Valuable Player in 1939, 1941, and 1947.

COURTESY HAWAII STATE ARCHIVES

Babe Ruth, Mrs. Ruth, and their daughter were welcomed to the islands by Duke—and 10,000 enthusi-
astic fans—in 1933. Ruth declared, "I'm ready to do anything you want, so long as it's playing golf."
His daughter asked to be taught to ride a board, and his wife planned on swimming. Babe played in
two exhibition games and thrilled the crowd with his home runs. He also signed hundreds of auto-
graphs.

The long-awaited day—August 24, 1990—Duke's statue at Waikīkī's Kūhiō Beach was dedicated on the centennial of his birth. It was immediately one of the most photographed attractions in Hawai'i.

How did the sculptor, Jan Fisher, decide how to depict Duke, a man of so many accomplishments?

Fisher said, "I wanted to capture Duke's 'essence.' The 17-1/2-foot bronze statue has Duke in his swimming trunks, because he was the world's champion swimmer for more than a decade, and revolutionized competitive swimming; with his longboard, because he's the Father of International Surfing; and he has a lei around his neck, with his arms outstretched, because he was the ambassador of Hawai'i to the world."

Nadine was invited to view and critique the statue. She scratched two lines on Duke's right thigh to indicate the correct length of his swimsuit trunks. The statue was cast with the marks still there.

———————◆———————

The statue became controversial. It was not lit. There were no plaques. Should the statue face the ocean?

Many beachboys were adamant that Duke would "Nevvah, nevvah turn his back on the ocean."

But if he faced the ocean, photographs would have an uninspiring background of high-rise buildings, which would not do Waikīkī justice. With his back to the ocean, a better photograph can be taken.

Nadine said: "I don't think he would really care. At least we finally got a statue."

———————◆———————

In steamship days, tourists would say their final aloha to Waikīkī as they steamed by, make a wish, then cast their leis overboard into the ocean.

Times have changed. Most tourists fly, but a tradition has started of tourists draping their leis on Duke's loving, outstretched arms as they bid aloha to Waikīkī.

Nadine said, "Duke would like that."

For four years after Duke's Waikīkī statue was in place, it had no identification, because of funding shortages. Tourists were puzzled. Many people joked that you had to go to California, Australia, or Florida to find out more about his accomplishments.

Hawai'i has many fine museums, including the Hawai'i Maritime Center and the Bishop Museum (a Polynesian culture museum), but ironically, there is no surfing museum. California boasts at least five, and there are several on the East Coast! The very popular Duke's Canoe Club Restaurant is a tourist mecca and acts as a quasi-museum.

PHOTO BY CARLOS VITI

Finally finished and with plaques in place, Duke's statue does what Duke did all his life: graciously welcome people to the ocean off Waikīkī.

Duke's Creed

In Hawai'i we greet friends, loved ones and strangers
with Aloha, which means with love.
Aloha is the key word to the universal spirit of real
hospitality, which makes Hawai'i renowned as the
world's center of understanding and fellowship.

Try meeting or leaving people with aloha.
You'll be surprised by their reaction.
I believe it and it is my creed.

Aloha to you.

Duke Paoa Kahanamoku

This message was printed on the back of his personal business card. His
message reaches thousands each week, as tourists stop to read it on a plaque
at the base of his statue at Waikīkī.

GLOSSARY

alaia
short, heavy surfboard

ali'i
chief; noble, royal

aloha
love, kindness, grace; also, "Farewell!"

'aumakua
ancestral spirits in animal form

chickenskin
Hawai'i term for the momentary roughness of skin known elsewhere as goose pimples or goose bumps

goofy foot
in surfing lingo, riding with the left foot at the back of the board

Great Mahele
Hawaiian land division, 1848

gremmies
in surfing lingo, young surfers

haole
Caucasian

Hawai'i *nei*
"this beloved Hawai'i"

he'e nalu
surfer, surfing

holo a i'a
to swim like a fish

hukilau
communal catching of fish with a net

humuhumunukunukuāpua'a
the triggerfish, the state fish of Hawai'i

kāhili
a staff topped with feathers, symbolic of royalty

kahu
honored attendant, guardian, adviser

kama'āina
native born

keiki
child

koa
wood used for making canoes, surfboards, bowls, and ukuleles

kupuna
learned and wise older person

makani
wind

malihini
stranger, foreigner, newcomer

Mele Kalīkimaka
Merry Christmas

'ohana
family

olo
long surfboard

Olympic Games, sequence
The modern Games began in 1896. Although they are normally scheduled every four years, in 1906 a special out-of-sequence Olympics was held to celebrate the Games' Greek history. Duke missed out on two possible Olympics: the 1916 Berlin Olympics, canceled because of World War I, and the 1928 Amsterdam Olympics, because he was ill.

outrigger canoe
a canoe with a shallow draught to navigate over reefs, used throughout the Pacific; the outrigger provides stability

pau
finished, all done

pīkake
jasmine flower; its tiny white flowers make a beautiful, fragrant lei

poi
a staple food, made from pounded taro root

skeg
surfboard fin

stoked
in surfing lingo, enthusiastic, exuberant

tandem
in surfing lingo, two people riding on a surfboard together, often in acrobatic positions

tūtū
any relative or close friend of grandparents' generation

INDEX

Entries in bold refer to photo captions.

ABOUT THE AUTHORS

Even though **Sandra Kimberley Hall** was born in Australia, Duke played a big part in her life. Some of her earliest memories are of stories about Duke's 1914 visit to Australia. She had pictured Duke arriving by surfboard at Freshwater, teaching the locals to surf, staying at her parents' home, and then paddling back to Hawai'i. After 23 years in Arizona, she moved to Hawai'i during the 1990 festivities surrounding Duke's centennial. Soon after, she met Duke's widow, one of her dearest friends now, and she decided it was time to find out the facts. Working freelance, she ascertained the details of Duke's visit to Australia, and became the consultant for the statue erected there for him in 1994. Her only disappointment was finding out that Duke did not stay at her family home!

A veteran researcher, Sandy has a Masters in Library Science from the University of Arizona, and for many years was the chief librarian at the *Arizona Daily Star*. She is a former director of the board of the Special Libraries Association and former chair of its News Division, as well as a member of the Historic Hawai'i Foundation, the Australian Society for Sports History, the North American Society for Sport History, and the Australian-American Chamber of Commerce. She has been a public relations consultant for 15 years, with clients worldwide.

With her children nearly launched, she is now exploring new paths, including high-altitude hiking in the Himalayas last year. This year she took her first surfing lesson and she is stoked! Her only wish is that she had surfed a long time ago.

Greg Ambrose, Honolulu journalist, surfer, and author of *Surfer's Guide to Hawaii* (Bess Press, 1991), reflects on the writing of *Memories of Duke*:

As I grew up in Hawai'i, the spirit of Duke Kahanamoku was everywhere. After he died, it was even more pronounced, a living, tangible thing that you could almost see. Duke's spirit is a way of interacting with the ocean with ease and comfort, and dealing with other people graciously. People speak of Duke as though he is still alive, as if they have surfed or swum or paddled with him just minutes ago.

I fell in love with the ocean the first moment I bodysurfed the shore break at Waikīkī. The passion grew deeper as I discovered diving, surfing, bodyboarding and sailing. I have never felt as happy as when in the comforting embrace of the sea.

As the ocean has become more crowded with people, I have often evoked the memory of Duke's calm dignity to try to ease my frustrations and cool my hot temper during the inevitable confrontations when too many wave riders fight over too few waves.

And now, I have the best job in the world at the *Honolulu Star-Bulletin*. I get to write about the ocean, all about the ocean. I get paid to try to make *kama'āina* and *malihini* alike appreciate what a treasure we have in our sea, and to realize that we all share the duty to protect and preserve it for our children. And as I write each story, I ask myself, what would Duke have thought about this? How would Duke have felt about this? Would Duke think this was a fair story? And I like to think that he would have enjoyed reading *Memories of Duke: The Legend Comes to Life*.

Working on this book has been a rare treat, to travel back in time with people who were fortunate to ride the waves with Duke, people who walked and talked with the man who more than anyone embodies aloha and what it means to be Hawaiian.